LOVE TO CROCHET PROJECTS

✝INTRODUCTION

I first learnt how to crochet ten years ago after watching my mother crocheting. I loved the simplicity and rhythm of crochet, working just one stitch at a time before moving onto the next. While I managed to pick up a very basic stitch simply by observing, I didn't make anything useful for quite a while. Instead I spent time playing around with basic increases and decreases, creating freeform shapes and three-dimensional bags. It felt wonderfully tactile. I had learnt to knit at quite a young age and so where I was used to knitting in rows and only seeing the shapes produced by increases and decreases after casting off, with crochet I could see what I was creating as I worked, altering the shapes as I went along. With crochet you can make absolutely any shape you can think of, as you are thinking it up.

As with any new technique, at first I found crochet a little fiddly. The hand positions used to hold the hook and yarn can feel alien to begin with, especially as you start with a single slip stitch and create everything from that one loop. With patience, persistence and practice, this awkward feeling quickly passes and anything becomes possible. There are only a few basic crochet stitches to learn and everything else is a variation on these few stitches. Once you are comfortable holding your hook and yarn, you will be well on your way with your colourful and exciting crochet journey.

The **LEARN TO CROCHET** projects in this book include some basic patterns – a good place to start if you haven't tried crochet before. These projects are small and manageable, designed to enable you to get familiar with the craft and the basic stitches. As you progress through the book the projects build in difficulty, introducing new techniques that will allow you to learn and practise new skills. Once you are comfortable with the basic crochet stitches, move on to the **LOVE TO CROCHET** projects. They may look a little daunting at first glance, but once you have mastered the basic stitches you will be able to make any of these garments. If you have crocheted before, feel free to jump in wherever you like. As some are larger garments or worked in finer yarns, these projects require greater concentration and are more time consuming. Do not panic if you make a mistake – the wonderful thing about crochet is that you'll only be working one stitch at a time so can you easily unravel your work to go back a couple of steps and redo where you went wrong.

As I learnt how to knit long before I attempted crochet, I find it difficult to talk about crocheting without mentioning knitting. I am often asked to compare the two. Which do I prefer? Which is better? It's more complicated than that. I can't say I prefer one over the other, but what I have learnt through practice is that, despite a few similarities, each craft produces different fabrics that lend themselves to different projects. Crochet is a wonderful and simple technique that, once mastered, can be used to create amazing garments, accessories and homewares really quickly. It's a very rhythmic craft and when you have the hang of the basic stitches, you'll have all the knowledge you need to make anything you like and then you can start exploring your own individual crochet style.

There is nothing more rewarding than making something by hand. Objects made by machine will never compare to your own creations. Whether it is for you or a loved one, a handmade garment will be cherished. I have loved designing and making every garment and accessory within this book. I hope that you too enjoy making these projects. Whether you are a complete beginner or have been crocheting for years, I hope this book becomes a part of your journey as a crocheter and that it inspires you to continue exploring other patterns, possibilities and maybe even designing your own projects.

+CROCHET BASICS

Unlike other crafts, crochet does not require a vast amount of specialist equipment. The only piece of kit that is absolutely essential for crochet is the hook, although a handful of other items will improve your work and make crocheting easier and more enjoyable.

CROCHET HOOKS are available in a variety of materials as well as sizes, colours and designs. Some come with grips for your fingers while others don't. As you practise crochet, you will discover the type of crochet hook that feels most comfortable in your hand. The size of the hook you need will depend on the thickness of the yarn you use. The smallest steel hooks designed for intricate lacework start at 0.75mm and go up to 3.5mm. The most commonly used hooks start at 3.5mm and go up to 10mm, but even larger plastic and wooden are available for supersized crochet. The hook's size correlates to the diameter measurement taken around the shank – the part of the crochet hook between the tip and throat and the grip. In the UK, this is given in millimetres. When checking a hook using a size guage, the shank should fit snugly into the correct size hole. Measurements do vary slightly depending on the manufacturer, so it is always sensible to crochet and measure a tension swatch (see pages 26–7) before beginning a project to ensure you are using the correct size hook.

IN YOUR BASIC CROCHET KIT YOU WILL ALSO NEED:

BLUNT-ENDED YARN OR TAPESTRY NEEDLE for stitching garment pieces together and weaving in loose yarn ends.

PEN AND PAPER for jotting down handy notes on your work as you follow a pattern.

PINS AND SAFETY PINS for pinning garment pieces together before you seam them to make sure everything stays in place.

SCISSORS for snipping yarns.

STEAM IRON for finishing and pressing.

STITCH MARKERS are useful for highlighting specific stitches or points in your work. You can use anything from safety pins to snippets of yarn that contrast in colour from the main working yarn. Alternatively, you can buy stitch markers that look like plastic safety pins.

TAPE MEASURE for checking tension and measuring the dimensions of garment pieces when necessary.

HOOK SIZES

METRIC	UK IMPERIAL	US
2mm	14	4 steel
2.25mm	13	B/1
2.5mm	12	1/0
2.75mm	11	C/2
3.25mm	10	D/3
3.5mm	9	E/4
3.75mm		F/5
4mm	8	G/6
4.5mm	7	7
5mm	6	H/8
5.5mm	5	I/9
6mm	4	J/10
6.5mm	3	K/10½
7mm	2	
8mm	0	L/11
9mm	00	M,N/13
10mm	000	N,P/15

CHOOSING YARNS

Yarns come in a vast range of colours, thicknesses and textures. There are some amazingly beautiful yarns out there – some of which have been hand dyed in vibrant colours and hand spun using locally sourced fibres. You will see yarns made from animal fibres, such as angora, alpaca, cashmere and wool, as well as plant fibres, including cotton, linen, hemp and even bamboo. As you become immersed in the craft of crochet, you will find yourself drawn to certain yarn types and colour shades. Experimenting with the different yarns available and developing your own crochet style can be a lot of fun. You will find that particular yarns cry out to be made into specific projects and that you must oblige. Other yarns will simply demand to be bought without projects immediately springing to mind. Over time you will get a good sense of what yarns work for which projects, as well as the thicknesses of yarn that you prefer to work with.

At the beginning of every crochet pattern, a recommended yarn is suggested along with the amount of this yarn needed for each size garment given in the pattern. This will be the yarn that the sample garment has been made up in and photographed. This doesn't mean that you can only use the recommended yarn for that pattern. You can use any yarn that you like as long as the tension achieved matches the tension stated at the beginning of the pattern.

Yarns generally come in universal weights or thicknesses, such as 4ply, double knitting, aran and chunky. The metreage or yardage and weight of your chosen yarn may differ to that of the yarn used in the pattern, so do be aware that you may need to buy more or fewer balls/hanks. Also be very careful to ensure that your tension matches that of the pattern when working with a different yarn. You may just need to tweak your hook size slightly.

YARN LABELS

Yarn labels carry a lot of information and so it's worth keeping hold of one per project just in case you need to refer back to any of that information, in particular the washing instructions. Usually, yarn labels contain the following:

BRAND NAME this is generally the name of the yarn manufacturer, which can be a global company, a local spinner or an individual designer.

YARN NAME this is usually an informative description including the weight of yarn but it may also be an evocative name.

YARN COMPOSITION this details which fibres the yarn is made up of and the amount much of each – this is commonly expressed as a percentage.

SHADE NAME OR NUMBER the colour of a yarn is often given as a name – which can be either straightforward or lyrical – but frequently it is expressed as a code number.

DYE LOT NUMBER this is an important number to be aware of as it denotes the batch in which the yarn has been dyed. Yarn is generally dyed in large batches and each lot is given its own individual code number that is printed on the yarn label. Often there is little difference between dye lots but sometimes yarn from separate batches can vary in shade. Before starting a project, make sure your yarn is from the same dye lot with identical codes. Ordinarily this isn't a problem as yarn shops and online retailers stock balls or hanks from the same dye lot. If you do run out of yarn midway through a project, you will need to have the dye lot number to hand so that you can request stock from the same batch when ordering more yarn.

WASHING INSTRUCTIONS this is essential information so you do not ruin a project that you have worked really hard on. Always pay close attention to the washing instructions given on a yarn label. If in doubt, hand wash the garment gently in cool water and allow it to dry flat.

RECOMMENDED NEEDLE/HOOK SIZE this gives a suggested crochet hook or knitting needle size for the weight of yarn.

TENSION this is the ideal number of stitches and rows to a specific area (usually 10cm square) when worked on a particular size crochet hook or knitting needle.

METREAGE/YARDAGE this states how many metres/yards of yarn are contained in an individual ball or hank of yarn.

WEIGHT this states how many grams/ounces of yarn are contained in an individual ball or hank of yarn.

READING PATTERNS

Once you have practised the basic crochet stitches, the next step is to understand how to work from patterns, learn the common abbreviations used in these patterns and bring all of these skills together. At first a crochet pattern can seem a little daunting with its apparent jumble of letters and numbers, but once you have taken a good look at the list of standard abbreviations on this page, it will all start to make more sense. Some patterns you encounter may be written out longhand with the terms explained in full, but it is more likely that the crochet patterns you see most often will be written using these abbreviations. It is important to take the time to read carefully through your pattern before you begin work so that you don't miss any important steps.

HOW TO READ A CROCHET PATTERN

The first word of a line of instruction lets you know whether you are working the stitches in a straight row or in a round. The first stitches to work are the beginning chain stitches that set up the row or round. The instructions will also tell you whether or not the chains are to be counted as your first stitch within your overall stitch count. These chains are worked to make sure that the first stitch of the row or round is going to be worked at the same height as the rest of the stitches. Any instructions given inside square brackets [ ] indicate that this is to be repeated the number of times given directly after the closing bracket or into the stitch specified. An asterisk means that the instructions that follow are then repeated by the number of times stated or to the end of the row or round. The instruction 'join' is usually used when working in the round and means you need to join the first and last stitches in the round with a slip stitch. The stitch counts given in brackets ( ) and italics after a line of instruction tell you how many stitches you should have worked in that specific row or round.

HOW TO WORK FROM A CROCHET STITCH DIAGRAM

Crochet patterns often come accompanied by a stitch diagram. At first these can look like assortments of shapes, but when you know what each symbol means, it can be really helpful to work from these diagrams. They provide more of a clear visual guide to what your finished crocheting should look like.

SYMBOLS

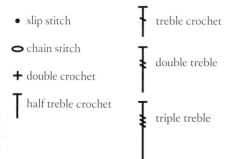

• slip stitch

⊙ chain stitch

✛ double crochet

⊤ half treble crochet

⊤ treble crochet

⊤ double treble

⊤ triple treble

ABBREVIATIONS

The following list shows the most commonly used abbreviations within crochet patterns. You'll see these shorthand terms popping up quite a lot so keep this list handy until you start to get used to these abbreviations.

alt	alternate
approx	approximately
beg	begin/beginning
bet	between
ch(s)	chain(s)
ch sp(s)	chain space(s)
cl	cluster(s)
cont	continue/continuing
dc	double crochet(s)
dec	decrease(s)/decreasing
dtr	double treble(s)
foll(s)	follow(s)/following
g	gram(s)
gr	group(s)
htr	half treble(s)
inc	increase(s)/increasing
lp(s)	loop(s)
patt(s)	pattern(s)
rem	remain(s)/remaining
rep(s)	repeat(s)/repeating
rnd(s)	round(s)
RS	right side
sc	single crochet
sp(s)	space(s)
sl st	slip stitch
st(s)	stitch(es)
tch	turning chain
tog	together
tr	treble(s)
trtr	triple treble(s)
WS	wrong side
yrh	yarn round hook
[ ]	work instructions within square bracket as many times as directed
( )	contains additional instruction or further clarification

When working from any crochet pattern, be very aware of whether the instructions are written using English or American crochet terminology. There is huge potential for confusion if you start working from an American crochet pattern without realising that some of the stitches are named differently. For example, the stitch known as 'treble crochet' in English terminology is actually referred to as 'double crochet' in an American pattern. All of the patterns in this book are written using English crochet terminology.

⁺STARTING OFF

SLIP KNOT

The starting point of any piece of crochet you make will be a slip knot, which will be your starting stitch. This first stitch will either be the first stitch of a foundation chain when working in rows or the first stitch of a base ring when working in the round. When making a slip knot you only really need to leave a short tail of yarn approximately 10cm (4in), which will be just long enough to stitch in the yarn end easily once you have finished crocheting. When counting your stitches, the initial slip knot always counts as the first 'cast-on' stitch.

STEP 1 Leaving a tail of approx 10cm (4in) long, curl the yarn into a loop.

STEP 2 With your crochet hook, enter the loop you have created and catch the working end of the yarn (the end attached to the ball of yarn) and pull through the centre of the loop. Pull gently on both ends of the yarn to tighten. You may now continue to make your foundation chain or base ring as per the pattern instructions you are following.

HOLDING THE HOOK AND YARN

Holding a crochet hook may feel strange at first and take a little practise before it feels comfortable, but with persistence you will soon be whizzing through patterns. As you learn to crochet, take the time to get the basic techniques right to ensure a neat tension. One hand holds the crochet hook, as though holding a pen or pencil. The other hand holds the working yarn and plays the role of feeding the hook with yarn, thereby determining the tension. There are two methods shown here for holding the yarn; try both to see which you prefer. The technique is the same whether you are left- or right-handed.

METHOD ONE Wrap the working yarn around your little finger and across your two middle fingers. Take the working yarn behind your index finger and to the front, leaving it to rest on your elevated index finger. There should be approximately 10cm (4in) between your index finger and the loop on your hook.

METHOD TWO (CONTINENTAL) This is another method that you can use if you find it most comfortable. Simply lie the working yarn across your palm and under your index finger and over. Wrap round once more. There should be approximately 10cm (4in) between your index finger and the loop on your hook.

YARN OVER AND CHAIN STITCH

The beginning of any crocheted fabric is nomally a length of chain stitches, so this chain stitch will be the first stitch that you learn and practise. Chains are also used at the ends of rows in order to take the hook up to the correct height before you start working on the next row. This is called a turning chain. It is important to keep the tension of your chain stitches even, neither too tight nor too loose, so that they are easy to insert the hook into when you work your next row or round.

STEP 1 With the slip knot sitting on the neck of your hook, hold the working yarn keeping a good tension on the tail end. Pass the hook from left to right under the working yarn, and around the yarn in an anticlockwise movement, to catch the yarn in the crook of the hook. This is called 'yarn round hook' (yrh).

STEP 2 Draw the working yarn through the slip knot or the stitch already on the hook. Keep the yarn under tension at all times. As you draw the working yarn through your loop, rotate the hook so that the crook is facing downwards. You have now made one new chain (ch). Repeat these two steps to create more chain stitches. To maintain a good tension on the yarn, you will need to reposition the fingers working the tension every four or five stitches.

COUNTING CHAINS

When counting chains, do not include the stitch or loop that is sitting on the hook. This is because a loop always remains on the hook right up to the point that you fasten off your work. To make it a bit easier to count chains when counting a large number, it is a good idea to place stitch markers at intervals, such as after every 10 or 20 stitches. Whenever possible, stitches should be counted from the front of the chain.

THE FRONT OF A CHAIN
The front of the chain will look like a series of V shapes. Each V is a chain loop sitting between two other chain loops. The first chain made will have the slip knot sitting directly before it. The surface of the chain is smooth on this front side.

THE REVERSE OF A CHAIN
The reverse of the chain has a row of bumps that sit behind the V and run in a straight line from the slip knot to the hook. The surface of the reverse of the chain is more textural than the front side.

✚WORKING IN ROWS

FIRST ROW

///

Working the first row of a crochet fabric can be a little fiddly as you will be working into each of the chains you have just worked on the foundation row. Depending on which crochet stitch you are working in, you will be instructed to skip a number of chains from the hook. The skipped chains will count as the first stitch and take your hook up to the correct height from the chain according to the stitch you are working in. Here we are working in double crochet (dc) so the first stitch is worked into the second chain from hook.

STEP 1 Skip the first chain and insert the hook into the second chain from the hook, into the centre of the V. (The number of chains skipped changes according to the crochet stitch being worked.) You can place your hook into the top side of the chain, thus working over just one yarn, or the lower part of the chain, thus working over two yarns. Working into the top side of the chain is the easiest method for a beginner, though it does result in a looser edge.

STEP 2 Wrap your working yarn from back to front over the hook. This is called 'yarn over' (yo).

STEP 3 Catch the working yarn with your hook and draw it through the chain to the front of your work.

STEP 4 Wrap your working yarn from back to front over the hook again.

STEP 5 Draw the yarn through both loops on the hook. One stitch has been completed. Repeat these steps to the end of the foundation row.

TURNING CHAINS

When you reach the end of any row and turn your work ready to begin the next row, you need to create a turning chain (tch) to bring your hook up to the correct height for the stitch to be worked along this row. Likewise, you must create turning chains when working in rounds.

The number of chains needed in a turning chain depends on the crochet stitch being first worked in that row or round. If your next stitch is double crochet (dc), your turning chain needs to be one chain. If you are working in half treble crochet (htr), your turning chain will be two chains. If you are working in treble crochet (tr), your turning chain must be three chains.

Making a turning chain is very simple. Create the number of chains you need by wrapping the working yarn round the hook (yrh) and drawing this yarn through the loop already on the hook. This counts as one chain. Repeat to make the requesite number of chains according to which stitch you are working in.

Unless otherwise stated, your turning chain is not counted as part of the overall stitch count. The next stitch in the row or round, however, will be worked into the second stitch along unless a pattern specifies that your next stitch is worked into the base of the turning chain.

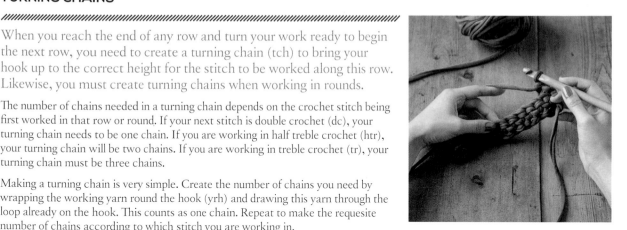

WORKING DOUBLE CROCHET

STEP 1 You will see that a row of Vs run along the top edge of your crochet. Once you have worked your turning chain, insert your hook under the next V along.

STEP 2 As with the first row, wrap the working yarn round the hook (yrh) and draw this yarn through the V so that you now have two loops sitting on your hook.

STEP 3 Wrap the working yarn round the hook again and draw it through both of the two loops on your hook. One double crochet has been completed. Repeat these steps to the end of the row.

⁺WORKING TREBLE CROCHET

Treble crochet (tr) is a longer stitch than double crochet (dc), so it forms a more open and therefore less dense fabric. As each individual stitch is longer, when working in treble crochet the fabric grows quickly. When working lacy stitch patterns, treble crochet is often used as the main stitch in combination with chains.

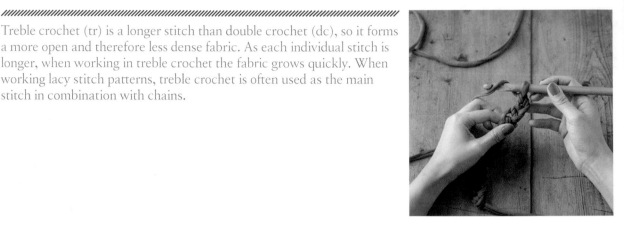

STEP 1 Work a foundation row consisting of the specified number of chains plus an additional three chains for the turning chain. As the turning chain is made up of three chains for treble crochet, the first stitch is worked into the fourth chain from the hook. Begin the first treble stitch by wrapping the working yarn round the hook.

STEP 2 Insert your hook into the fourth chain from the hook if working your first row or into the next stitch (V) along if working your second row or any subsequent row.

STEP 3 Pass the hook from left to right, or anticlockwise, under the working yarn to catch the yarn in the hook again.

STEP 4 Draw the yarn through the stitch or chain so there are now three loops sitting on your hook.

STEP 5 Wrap the working yarn round the hook again, as in step 3.

STEP 6 Draw the yarn through the first two loops on the hook, so there are now two loops sitting on your hook.

STEP 7 Wrap the working yarn round the hook again and draw it through the remaining two loops on the hook.

STEP 8 One treble crochet has been completed. Repeat these steps to the end of the row, beginning by wrapping the yarn round the hook and inserting it into the next foundation chain or next stitch along as in step 2.

+WORKING HALF TREBLE CROCHET

STEP 1 Work a foundation row consisting of the specified number of chains plus an additional two chains for the turning chain. As the turning chain is made up of two chains for half treble crochet, the first stitch is worked into the third chain from the hook. Begin the first half treble stitch by wrapping the working yarn round the hook.

STEP 2 Insert your hook into the third chain from the hook if working your first row or into the next stitch (V) along if working your second row or any subsequent row.

STEP 3 Pass the hook from left to right, or anticlockwise, under the working yarn to catch the yarn in the hook again.

STEP 4 Draw the yarn through the stitch or chain so there are now three loops sitting on your hook.

STEP 5 Wrap the working yarn round the hook again, as in step 3.

STEP 6 Draw the yarn through all three loops on the hook. One half treble has been completed. Repeat these steps to the end of the row, beginning by wrapping the yarn round the hook and inserting it into the next foundation chain or next stitch along as in step 2.

FASTENING OFF

It is very easy to fasten off a
piece of crochet. Once you
have completed your final stitch
you will have just one loop
remaining on the hook. Snip the
working yarn leaving a tail of
approximately 10cm (4in). Using
your fingers, loosen the loop of the
final stitch and carefully remove
it from the hook. Pass the tail of
yarn through this final stitch loop
and gently pull the tail end to close
the loop and secure the stitch.

✝WORKING IN THE ROUND

SLIP STITCH

//

When you work in the round you will often start with a foundation chain that is then joined by a slip stitch (sl st) to form the foundation ring.

STEP 1 To join your foundation chain into a ring, insert the hook from the front to the back of the first chain made.

STEP 2 Wrap the working yarn round the hook.

FIRST ROUND

STEP 3 Draw the working yarn through both the chain and the loop on the hook.

STEP 4 You will now have one loop on the hook and the foundation ring has been formed. Chain one before you begin the next round; this chain counts as your first stitch. The number of chains you make will depend on the stitch you are working in.

STEP 1 Insert the hook from front to back into the very centre space of the foundation ring. Wrap the working yarn round the hook.

STEP 2 Draw the yarn through so you have two loops sitting on your hook. Wrap the working yarn round hook once more.

STEP 3 Draw the yarn through both loops sitting on your hook. There is now one loop on the hook and one double crochet stitch has been made.

STEP 4 Repeat this until the required number of stitches have been worked into the centre of the foundation ring.

STEP 5 To join the first round together with a slip stitch, insert your hook into the first stitch of the round.

STEP 6 Wrap the working yarn round the hook.

STEP 7 Draw the yarn through the stitch and the loop already on the hook. One full round has been completed.

✛INCREASING STITCHES

INCREASING IN THE ROUND

When working in the round, to produce a nice flat circle you will find that you need to increase (inc) at certain points. Increasing is really simple and just means that you are increasing the number of stitches in each round, making the circumference larger.

STEP 1 Make your chain at the beginning of the round, and work your first stitch into the next stitch along. Wrap the working yarn round the hook.

STEP 2 To increase by one stitch, you simply need to work two stitches into the same space. So, insert your hook back into the base of the stitch that you have just worked and make a second stitch in the same way as the first.

INCREASING IN ROWS

Increasing stitches (inc) when working in rows of crochet uses exactly the same method as increasing while working in the round. You simply work two or more crochet stitches into a single stitch from the row below.

STEP 3 Wrap the working yarn round the hook, draw the yarn through to the front of the work.

STEP 4 Complete the treble crochet stitch by wrapping the yarn round the hook and passing through two of the loops on your hook, wrap the yarn round the hook again and draw the yarn through all the remaining loops to finish your stitch. You will see that you have increased by working two stitches into one stitch from the row below.

DOUBLE CROCHET DECREASE

Decreasing (dec) by one stitch at a time is really simple and decreases are usually made by working two stitches together. The decreasing method changes slightly depending on which crochet stitch you are working in. The method shown below is working two double crochets together to make one stitch from two. The abbreviation for this is dc2tog.

STEP 1 To decrease, insert your hook into the next stitch, wrap the working yarn round the hook and draw the loop through. You now have two loops on your hook.

STEP 2 Instead of wrapping the yarn round the hook and drawing it through the remaining loops to finish the double crochet stitch, insert your hook into the next stitch along, wrap the yarn round the hook and draw through the stitch so that you have three loops sitting on your hook.

STEP 3 Wrap the working yarn round the hook once more and draw the yarn through all three of the loops on your hook. One double crochet has now been decreased.

⁺HALF TREBLE DECREASE

A half treble decrease to create one stitch from two stitches is worked in a very similar way to the double crochet decrease, in that you work half the stitch, then move onto the next stitch before drawing them both together to form one stitch. The abbreviation for this decrease is htr2tog.

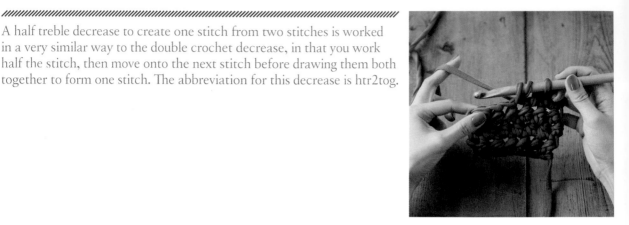

STEP 1 To decrease when working in half treble crochet (htr), wrap the working yarn round the hook, insert the hook into the next stitch, yarn rround hook again and then draw the yarn through the stitch so you have three loops sitting on your hook.

STEP 2 Instead of continuing and finishing the half treble stitch as you usually would, wrap the yarn round the hook again and insert your hook into the next stitch along.

STEP 3 Wrap the yarn round the hook again and draw the yarn through the stitch so there are now five loops sitting on your hook.

STEP 4 Yarn round hook once more, then draw the yarn all the way through all the five loops sitting on your hook. You have now completed your decrease and one half treble crochet stitch has been decreased.

⁺TREBLE DECREASE

STEP 1 Wrap the working yarn round the hook, insert the hook into the next stitch, wrap the yarn round the hook once more and draw the yarn through to the front of the work so that you now have three loops on your hook.

STEP 2 Wrap the yarn round the hook again then draw the yarn through two of the loops that are on your hook.

STEP 3 There are now two loops on your hook.

STEP 4 Wrap the yarn round your hook again and insert your hook into the next stitch along.

STEP 5 Yarn round hook again and draw yarn through to the front of your work so you now have four loops sitting on your crochet hook. Yarn round hook again and then draw the yarn through two of the loops on your hook.

STEP 6 You now have three loops on your crochet hook. Finally, yarn round hook once more and draw yarn through all three of the remaining loops on your hook. You have now completed your decrease and one treble crochet stitch has been decreased. The abbreviation for this decrease is tr2tog.

⁺ABRUPT DECREASE

Most of the time, when you're crocheting, you will find that most decreases (decs) are made gradually – by turning two stitches into one. However, you will occasionally need to decrease abruptly at the side of your work when working armhole shaping for example. You will only need to work this abrupt decrease at the beginning of a row, as if you need to decrease abruptly at the end of a row, simply stop the row early by however many stitches you require and turn, shortening your row.

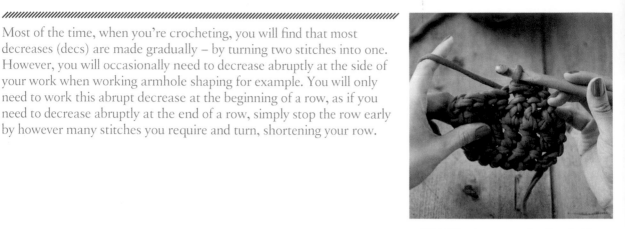

STEP 1 Begin your row by slip stitching along the number of stitches required to make your abrupt decrease. Slip stitches are the shortest crochet stitches so this makes them ideal for moving across a row without your work growing in length.

STEP 2 When you have worked your slip stitches, you will then need to make a chain to bring your hook up to the correct height. The number of chains will depend on which crochet stitch you're working in.

STEP 3 Work your next stitch as normal in your crochet stitch pattern.

STEP 4 Continue to the end of the row. You will be able to see your abrupt decrease at the beginning of your row.

JOINING IN A NEW COLOUR

IN THE MIDDLE OF A ROW

STEP 1 The method for changing colour is the same whether you're working in rows or rounds. You need to plan ahead slightly as you will begin your colour change the stitch before. When working the final stitch before your colour change, stop before the final yarn round hook. Cut the old colour yarn, leaving a long tail. Leaving a long tail, loop your new colour yarn around your hook.

STEP 2 Draw the new colour yarn through the remaining loops on your hook to finish off the stitch. Gently pull the old and new colour yarn ends to tighten the loop on the hook. Changing colour will create yarn ends which you can either weave into the back of your work afterwards or you can work them in with your crocheting of the next few stitches to fasten them in place.

STEP 3 Now that you have fastened in your new colour, continue to work the rest of the row in the new colour yarn according to the pattern instructions that you are following.

AT THE END OF A ROW

STEP 1 The method for changing colour at the end of a row is similar to changing colour in the middle of row as you must plan ahead. Before you work the final yarn round hook of the final stitch of the row, cut your old colour yarn leaving a long tail and loop your new colour yarn around the hook.

STEP 2 Draw your new colour yarn through the remaining two loops on your hook to finish off the final stitch of that row. Gently pull the old and new colour yarn ends to tighten the loop on the hook.

VSTEP 3 Continue to work in your crochet pattern, beginning with your turning chain to start the next row. Then, just work the rest of the row in your new colour according to your pattern instructions.

⁺MATTRESS STITCH

Mattress stitch is a great stitch to learn as it leaves you with really neat seams that are almost unnoticeable. What I really love about mattress stitch is that it is worked with the right sides of the fabric facing out towards you so, as you stitch, you can keep an eye on how your work will look on the outside.

To work mattress stitch, lay your two pieces of crochet that you would like to seam together on a flat surface with the right sides facing upwards. With a tapestry needle begin by stitching down into the fabric on your right hand side, a few millimetres from the seam edge. Then stitch upwards into the fabric on your left hand side, then down into this fabric a few millimetres up, then

upwards into the fabric on your right hand side, then down into this fabric again a few millimetres up. Repeat this for a few stitches and then gently pull each end of the yarn that you're working with the tighten up your seam. Continue to work like this along the full length of the seam and then weave in the ends of your yarn into the back of your work.

Making tension swatches can seem a bit painstaking to begin with, but they're incredibly important, especially if you are a beginner crocheter. There might be a few projects that you can get away with jumping head first in without doing a tension swatch, such as accessories or if you're working on a homewares project – any projects where the measurements don't need to be strictly precise.

If you're making a garment, however, definitely force yourself to make a tension swatch first. This way you can ensure that your tension matches the tension of the pattern and therefore you will be able to make your garment to the precise size that you would like and it will fit you properly. As you become a more experienced crocheter you will get an idea of what your tension is usually like and whether you need to go up or down a hook size to reach the required tension. You'll get quickier working up tension swatches and matching the tension given on the pattern.

The tension given at the beginning of a crochet pattern is usually written by giving the number of stitches and rows in a 10cm (4in) square. If a project is to be crocheted up in quite a

chunky yarn then the tension may be given over a larger area just so it's more of a precise measurement. It's best to crochet a slightly bigger square than 10cm (4in), by a few centimetres or an inch extra, so that you can take your tension measurement from the centre of your swatch.

When you have crocheted a good sized swatch, lay it out on a flat surface, take a tape measure and use pins to mark out a 10cm (4in) square then count the stitches and rows within this square. Once you have counted your stitches and rows you can compare your tension to that given on the pattern.

If your tension matches that given at the beginning of the pattern, then that's great! Your garment will crochet up to the exact size required. If your tension doesn't match, don't worry. If you find that you have more stitches within the 10cm than the pattern states this means that your tension is too tight so try working another tension swatch using a slightly thicker crochet hook. If you find that you have fewer stitches within the 10cm then this means that your tension is to loose so try working another tension swatch using a slightly thinner hook. It may seem a little painstaking, but it's definitely worth getting right.

+BUTTONHOLES

HORIZONTAL

STEP 1 Buttonholes normally sit a few stitches in from the edge of the garment. Work your stitch until you reach the point you'd like to position your buttonhole, then chain the number of stitches to correspond with the size of the button. Make sure the buttonhole is slightly smaller than the button so that the fastening stays firmly closed.

STEP 2 Skip the same number of stitches as the number of chains you have just made, then work into the next stitch as normal. This chain bridges the gap over your skipped stitches and you have created a buttonhole.

STEP 3 Crochet to the end of the row as usual. When you work the next row, work as normal and until you reach the chain-space, crochet the same number of stitches into the chain-space as were skipped. As this stage, test the hole with your button – it should go through relatively easily but not too loosely. If the hole isn't right, rework.

VERTICAL

STEP 1 Vertical buttonholes are worked by dividing the piece of crochet into two sections at the position of the buttonhole and working the same number of rows on each side, then join the two sides up afterwards. To begin, work in your stitch pattern to the point you would like to make a buttonhole, turn and work on these stitches to this side of your buttonhole until you have worked the length you would like your buttonhole.

STEP 2 Break your yarn and, miss one stitch at the point of your buttonhole, rejoin your yarn and work to the end of the row. Work just on these stitches on one side of the buttonhole until you have worked the same number of rows as on the other side of the buttonhole. Work up to the point of the buttonhole, chain one, and then join to the other side by continuing to work along those stitches to the end of the row.

STEP 3 When working the next row, when you reach the chain-space you've just created at the buttonhole, crochet one stitch into the chain space to make up for the stitch you skipped in the row below. Test the hole with your button to ensure that the size is correct. You want your button to go through relatively easily but not to slide through.

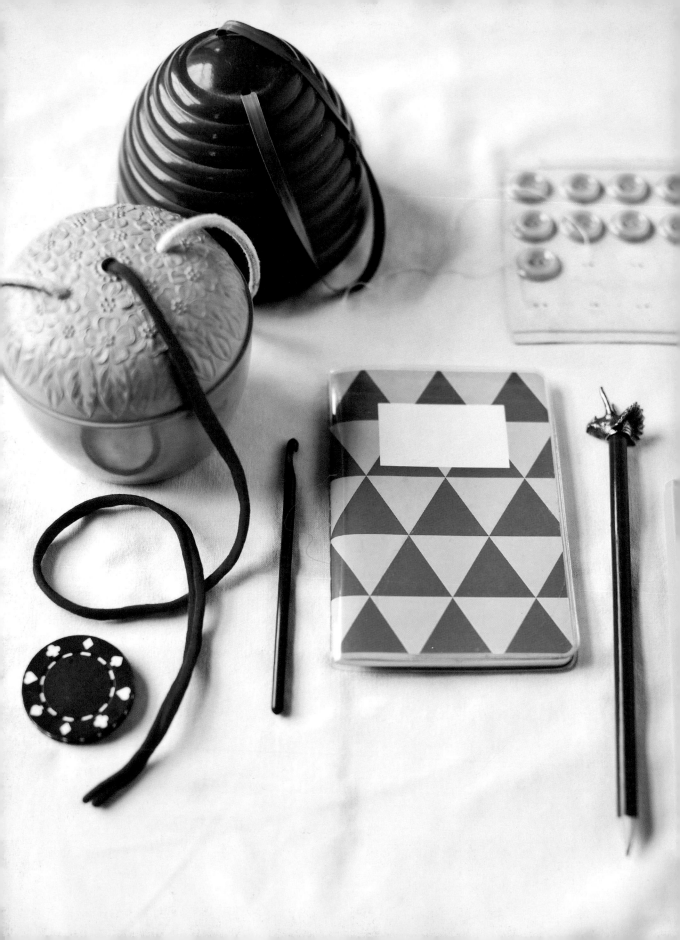

LEARN TO CROCHET

SIMPLE WRISTWARMERS

//

YOU WILL NEED

YARN

For one pair of plain wristwarmers
2 x 25g (⅞oz) balls of Jamieson's of Shetland *Spindrift*,
or a similar 4ply-weight wool yarn, in one colour, such as
mustard (1160 Scotch Broom)

For one pair of striped wristwarmers
1 x 25g (⅞oz) ball of Jamieson's of Shetland *Spindrift* and
JC Rennie *Supersoft Lambswool 4ply*, or a similar 4ply-
weight wool yarn, in each of four colours:
A green-blue (769 Willow)
B charcoal (109 Black/Shaela)
C pale pink (268 Dog Rose)
D dark red (380 Blaze)

For one pair of blue and mustard wristwarmers
1 x 25g (⅞oz) ball of Jamieson's of Shetland *Spindrift* and
JC Rennie *Supersoft Lambswool 4ply*, or a similar 4ply-
weight wool yarn, in each of four colours:
A charcoal (109 Black/Shaela)
B mustard (1160 Scotch Broom)
C mid-blue (136 Teviot)
D dark red (380 Blaze)

CROCHET HOOKS
4mm and 5mm (US sizes G/6 and H/8) crochet hooks

OTHER EQUIPMENT
Blunt-ended needle or tapestry needle for weaving in yarn
ends and seaming

TENSION
18 sts and 20 rows to 10cm (4in) measured over half
treble crochet using a 4mm (US size G/6) crochet hook

ABBREVIATIONS
See page 9

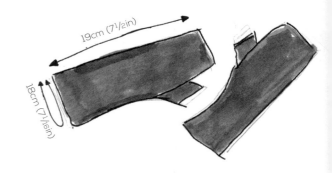

19cm (7½in)

18cm (7¹⁄₁₆in)

blue and mustard wristwarmers

///

TO MAKE THE PLAIN WRISTWARMERS

Foundation chain: Using 5mm (US size H/8) hook, make 32 chain + 2 chain.

Change to a 4mm (US size G/6) hook and cont working in rows, turning at end of each row.

Row 1: 1 htr in third ch from hook, 1 htr in each of next 5 ch, *work a dec by working 2 sts tog to make 1 st (htr2tog), 1 htr in next 6 ch; rep from * to end of row, dec one more st by missing last st, turn. *(28 sts)*

Row 2: 2 ch, 1 htr in each of next 4 sts, *htr2tog, 1 htr in next 5 sts; rep from * to end of row, dec one more st by missing last st, turn. *(24 sts)*

Rows 3–5: 2 ch, 1 htr in each st to end of row, turn.

Rows 6–7: 2 ch, inc 1 st at beg of row by working 1 htr in base of st just worked, 1 htr in each st to end of row, turn. *(26 sts)*

Rows 8–12: 2 ch, 1 htr in each st to end of row, turn.

Rows 13–16: 2 ch, inc 1 st at beg of row by working 1 htr in base of st just worked, 1 htr in each st to end of row, turn. *(30 sts)*

Cont working in rows, but at the same time place markers on Rows 20 and 26 to indicate position of thumbholes when seaming.

Rows 17–28: 2 ch, 1 htr in each st to end of row.

Rows 29–30: 2 ch, htr2tog, 1 htr in each st to end of row. *(29 sts)*

Rows 31–32: 2 ch, 1 htr in each st to end of row.

Rows 33–34: 2 ch, htr2tog, 1 htr in each st to end of row. *(28 sts)*

Row 35: 2 ch, 1 htr in each st to end of row.

Rows 36–37: 2 ch, htr2tog, 1 htr in each st to end of row. *(27 sts)*

Break yarn and fasten off.

TO FINISH

Weave any loose yarn ends into the back of your work so they are not visible from the right side.

Lightly steam all the garment pieces.

Sew the sides of the wristwarmer together to form a tube, leaving an opening between the markers placed at Rows 20 and 26 for the thumbholes. Take care not to stitch the cuff too tightly so you can easily slide your hand in and out.

WORK THE THUMBHOLES

Beg at centre top of each thumbhole, 2 ch, work 10 htr evenly along each side of wristwarmer around thumbhole, ending back at centre top, join rnd with a sl st in top of 2-ch to make a ring. *(20 sts)*

Cont to work in rounds, with RS always facing.

Round 1: 2 ch (counts as first htr), 1 htr in each of next 7 sts, [htr2tog] twice, 1 htr in each of next 8 sts. *(18 sts)*

Round 2: 2 ch (counts as first htr), 1 htr in each of next 6 sts, [htr2tog] twice, 1 htr in each of next 7 sts. *(16 sts)*

Round 3: 2 ch (counts as first htr), 1 htr in each of next 5 sts, [htr2tog] twice, 1 htr in each of next 6 sts. *(14 sts)*

Round 4: 2 ch (counts as first htr), 1 htr in each of next 4 sts, [htr2tog] twice, 1 htr in each of next 5 sts. *(12 sts)*

Round 5: 2 ch (counts as first htr), 1 htr in each of next 3 sts, [htr2tog] twice, 1 htr in each of next 4 sts *(10 sts)*.

Break yarn and fasten off. Weave in any loose yarn ends.

TO MAKE THE STRIPED WRISTWARMERS

Work as given for the pair of plain wristwarmers but using the following stripe pattern:

FIRST WRISTWARMER

Rows 1–5: Col C.

Rows 6–7: Col B.

Rows 8–10: Col C.

Rows 11–17: Col A.

Rows 18–19: Col B.

Rows 20–22: Col C.

Row 23: Col D.

Rows 24–25: Col C.

Row 26: Col D.

Rows 27–30: Col A.

Rows 31–35: Col B.

Row 36: Col C.

Row 37: Col D.

Work thumbholes in Col D.

SECOND WRISTWARMER
Rows 1–9: Col A.
Rows 10–11: Col B.
Rows 12–16: Col C.
Row 17: Col B.
Row 18: Col C.
Rows 19–20: Col D.
Row 21: Col A.
Rows 22–24: Col B.
Rows 25–29: Col C.
Rows 30–32: Col D.
Rows 33–35: Col A.
Row 36: Col B.
Row 37: Col A.
Work thumbholes in Col A until end of Round 3.
Work thumbholes Rounds 4–5 in Col B.

TO MAKE THE BLUE AND MUSTARD STRIPED WRISTWARMERS
Both wristwarmers are made using the same stitch pattern, but following different stripe patterns as follows:

FIRST WRISTWARMER
Rows 1–4: Col A.
Rows 5–15: Col C.
Row 16: Col D.
Rows 17–19: Col C.
Rows 20–21: Col A.
Rows 22–28: Col B.
Rows 29–30: Col A.
Rows 31–35: Col C.

SECOND WRISTWARMER
Rows 1–17: Col B.
Rows 18–19: Col A.

Rows 20–23: Col C.
Rows 24–25: Col A.
Rows 26–27: Col D.
Row 28: Col C.
Rows 29–35: Col B.

Using a 5mm (US size H/8) hook, make 41 chain + 2 chain. Change to a 4mm (US size G/6) hook.
Cont working in rows, turning at end of each row.
Row 1: 1 htr in third ch from hook, *1 htr in next st; rep from * to end of row. *(41 sts)*
Row 2: 2 ch, 1 htr in next st and foll 6 sts, *work a dec by working 2 sts tog to make 1 st (htr2tog), 1 htr in next 8 sts; rep from * to end of row, dec one more st at end of row by missing last st, turn. *(36 sts)*
Row 3: 2 ch, 1 htr in each st to end of row.
Row 4: 2 ch, 1 htr in each of next 6 sts, *htr2tog, 1 htr in each of next 7 sts; rep from * to end of row. *(33 sts)*
Rows 5–12: 2 ch, 1 htr in each st to end of row.
Rows 13–21: Cont to work in htr patt but inc first at beg of each row by 1 htr in same st as 2-ch. *(42 sts)*
Rows 22–29: 2 ch, 1 htr in each st to end of row.
Rows 30–35: 2 ch, htr2tog, 1 htr in each st to end of row. *(36 sts)*
Break yarn and fasten off.

TO FINISH
Weave any loose yarn ends into the back of your work so they are not visible from the right side.
Lightly steam all the garment pieces.
Sew the sides of the wristwarmer together to form a tube, leaving an opening towards the top edge of approximately 4cm (1½in) long for the thumbholes. Take care not to stitch the cuff too tightly so you can easily slide your hand in and out.

SNOOD AND HEADBAND

YOU WILL NEED

YARN
2 x 50g (1¾oz) balls of Orkney Angora *St Magnus DK*, or a similar double-knitting-weight wool yarn, in one colour:
A bright red (Scarlet)
1 x 50g (1¾oz) ball of Orkney Angora *St Magnus DK*, or a similar double-knitting-weight wool yarn, in each of two colours:
B mustard (Magical Goose)
C pale blue (Aqua)

CROCHET HOOK
4mm (US size G/6) crochet hook

OTHER EQUIPMENT
Blunt-ended needle or tapestry needle for weaving in yarn ends and seaming

TENSION
7½ cluster repeats and 16 rows to 10cm (4in) measured over stitch pattern using a 4mm (US size G/6) crochet hook

ABBREVIATIONS
See page 9

SNOOD:
Foundation chain: Using a 4mm (US size G/6) hook and Col A, make 124 chain + 1 chain.
Cont working in rows, turning at end of each row.
Row 1: 1 dc in second ch from hook, 1 dc in each ch to end of row. *(124 sts)*
Row 2: Change to Col C, 1 ch, 1 dc in st at base of ch, *2 ch, miss 2 sts, 1 dc in next st; rep from * to end of row.
Row 3: Change to Col A, 3 ch, 1 tr in st at base of ch, *miss 2 sts, 3tr in next st; rep from * to end of row, ending last rep with 2 tr in last st.
Row 4: Change to Col A, work as Row 2.
Row 5: Change to Col B, work as Row 3.
Row 6: Change to Col A, work as Row 2.
Row 7: Change to Col A, work as Row 3.
Row 8: Change to Col C, work as Row 2.
Row 9: Change to Col A, work as Row 3.
Row 10: Change to Col C, work as Row 2.
Row 11: Change to Col B, work as Row 3.
Row 12: Change to Col C, work as Row 2.
Row 13: Change to Col A, work as Row 3.
Row 14: Change to Col C, work as Row 2.
Row 15: Change to Col A, work as Row 3.
Row 16: Change to Col A, work as Row 2.
Row 17: Change to Col B, work as Row 3.
Row 18: Change to Col A, work as Row 2.
Row 19: Change to Col A, work as Row 3.
Row 20: Change to Col C, work as Row 2.
Row 21: Change to Col A, work as Row 3.
Row 22: Change to Col C, work as Row 2.
Row 23: Change to Col B, work as Row 3.
Row 24: Change to Col C, work as Row 2.
Row 25: Change to Col A, work as Row 3.
Row 26: Change to Col C, work as Row 2.
Row 27: Change to Col A , work as Row 3.
Row 28: Change to Col A, work as Row 2.
Row 29: Change to Col B, work as Row 3.
Row 30: Change to Col A, work as Row 2.
Row 31: Change to Col A, work as Row 3.
Row 32: Change to Col C, work as Row 2.
Row 33: Change to Col A, work as Row 3.
Break yarn and fasten off.

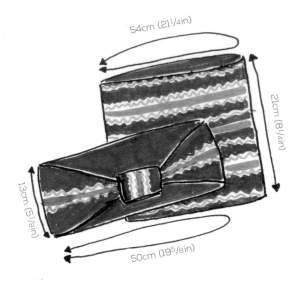

54cm (21¼in)

21cm (8¼in)

13cm (5⅛in)

50cm (19⅝in)

MAIN HEADBAND

Using a 4mm (US size G/6) crochet hook and Col A, make 107 chain + 1 chain.

Cont working in rows, turning at end of each row.

Row 1: 1 dc in second ch from hook, 1 dc in each ch to end of row. *(107 sts)*

Row 2: 1 ch, 1 dc in st at base of ch, *2 ch, miss 2 sts, 1 dc in next st; rep from * to end of row.

Row 3: 3 ch, 1 tr in st at base of ch, *miss 2 sts, 3 tr in next st; rep from * to end of row, ending last rep with 2 tr in last st.

Row 4: Work as Row 2.

Row 5: Change to Col B, work as Row 3.

Row 6: Change to Col A, work as Row 2.

Row 7: Change to Col A, work as Row 3.

Row 8: Change to Col C, work as Row 2.

Row 9: Change to Col A, work as Row 3.

Row 10: Change to Col C, work as Row 2.

Row 11: Change to Col B, work as Row 3.

Row 12: Change to Col C, work as Row 2.

Row 13: Change to Col A, work as Row 3.

Row 14: Change to Col C, work as Row 2.

Row 15: Change to Col A, work as Row 3.

Row 16: Change to Col A, work as Row 2.

Row 17: Change to Col B, work as Row 3.

Row 18: Change to Col A, work as Row 2.

Row 19: Change to Col A, work as Row 3.

Row 20: Change to Col A, work as Row 2.

Break yarn and fasten off.

SMALLER BAND

Using a 4mm (US size G/6) crochet hook and Col A, make 27 chain + 1 chain.

Cont working in rows, turning at end of each row.

Row 1: 1 dc in second ch from hook, 1 dc in each ch to end of row. *(107 sts)*

Row 2: 1 ch, 1 dc in st at base of ch, *2 ch, miss 2 sts, 1 dc in next st; rep from * to end of row.

Row 3: 3 ch, 1 tr in st at base of ch, *miss 2 sts, 3 tr in next st; rep from * to end of row, ending last rep with 2 tr in last st.

Row 4: Change to Col C, work as Row 2.

Row 5: Change to Col A, work as Row 3.

Row 6: Change to Col C, work as Row 2.

Row 7: Change to Col B, work as Row 3.

Row 8: Change to Col C, work as Row 2.

Row 9: Change to Col A, work as Row 3.

Row 10: Change to Col C, work as Row 2.

Row 11: Change to Col A, work as Row 3.

Row 12: Change to Col A, work as Row 2.

Break yarn and fasten off.

TO FINISH

Weave any loose yarn ends into the back of your work so they are not visible from the right side.

Lightly steam all the garment pieces.

Stitch the two short sides of the main band together to form a loop. Next stitch the two short sides of the smaller band together, encasing the larger main band as you sew, hiding the seam of the main band.

+BULLSEYE
CLUTCH BAGS

SIZE: **ONE SIZE**

//

YOU WILL NEED

YARN

Colourway A

1 x 50g (1¾oz) ball of Rico Creative Cotton *Aran*, or a similar aran-weight wool yarn, in each of three colours:

A pale orange (76 Tangerine)
B dark blue (38 Dark Blue)
C ecru (60 Natural)

Colourway B

1 x 50g (1¾oz) ball of Rico Creative Cotton *Aran*, or a similar aran-weight wool yarn, in each of four colours:

A pale orange (76 Tangerine)
B orange (74 Orange)
C bright pink (13 Fuchsia)
D purple (11 Cardinal)

Colourway C

1 x 50g (1¾oz) ball of Rico Creative Cotton *Aran*, or a similar aran-weight wool yarn, in each of two colours:

A orange (74 Orange)
B bright blue (39 Royal)

Only a small amount of each colour yarn is required for one bag, so to make all three clutch bags only 1 x 50g (1¾oz) ball of each of the separate colours is needed.

CROCHET HOOK
4.5mm (US size 7) crochet hook

OTHER MATERIALS
18cm (7in) zipper, for each bag
Lining fabric (optional)
Sewing thread in a matching colour, for stitching lining into the bag (optional)

OTHER EQUIPMENT
Blunt-ended needle or tapestry needle, for stitching together the bag
Sewing needle, for stitching the lining into the bag

TENSION
9–10 sts and 5 rounds to 5cm (2in) measured over treble crochet using a 4.5mm (US size 7) crochet hook

ABBREVIATIONS
See page 9

colourway c

colourway b

FRONT AND BACK PANELS (MAKE 2)

The Front and Back panels of all the bags are made using the same stitch pattern, but following different stripe sequences as folls:

Colourway A stripe sequence

FRONT AND BACK

Rounds 1, 4 and 7: Col A.
Rounds 2, 5 and 8: Col B.
Rounds 3 and 6: Col C.
Bag Strap: Col B.

Colourway B stripe sequences

FRONT

Rounds 1 and 2: Col A.
Rounds 3 and 4: Col B.
Rounds 5 and 6: Col C.
Rounds 7 and 8: Col D.

BACK

Rounds 1 and 2: Col D.
Rounds 3 and 4: Col C.
Rounds 5 and 6: Col B.
Rounds 7 and 8: Col A.
Bag Strap: Col D.

Colourway C stripe sequences

FRONT

Rounds 1, 2, 5 and 6: Col A.
Rounds 3, 4, 7 and 8: Col B.

BACK

Rounds 1, 2, 5 and 6: Col B.
Rounds 3, 4, 7 and 8: Col A.
Bag Strap: Col A.

FRONT AND BACK PANELS STITCH PATTERN

Changing colours where indicated above, work as folls:

Foundation ring: Using a 4.5mm (US size 7) crochet hook, make 4 chain, join with a sl st in first ch to make a ring.

Cont working in rounds, with RS always facing.

Round 1: 3 ch (counts as first tr), [1tr] 11 times in centre of ring, join with a sl st in top of 3-ch. *(12sts)*

Round 2: 3 ch (counts as first tr), 1 tr in base of 3-ch to make first inc, 2 tr in each st to end of rnd, join with a sl st in top of 3-ch. *(24 sts)*

Round 3: 3 ch (counts as first tr), 2 tr in next st, *1 tr in next st, 2 tr in foll st; rep from * to end of rnd, join with a sl st in top of 3-ch. *(36 sts)*

Round 4: 3 ch (counts as first tr), 1 tr in next st, 2 tr in foll st, *1 tr in each of next 2 sts, 2 tr in foll st; rep from * to end of rnd, join with a sl st in top of 3-ch. *(48 sts)*

Round 5: 3 ch (counts as first tr), 1 tr in next 2 sts, 2 tr in foll st, *1 tr in each of next 3 sts, 2 tr in foll st; rep from * to end of rnd, join with a sl st in top of 3-ch. *(60 sts)*

Rounds 6–8: Cont in patt as set, inc number of single tr sts between each inc by 1 st each rnd, so at end of each rnd the number of sts is inc by 12. *(96 sts)*

Break yarn and fasten off, leaving tail of at least 10cm (4 in).

STRAP

Using a 4.5mm (US size 7) crochet hook, make 49 chain + 1 chain.

Cont working in rows, turning at end of each row.

Row 1: 1 dc in second ch from hook, 1 dc in each ch to end of row. *(49 sts)*

Row 2: 2 ch (counts as first dc), 1dc in each st to end of row.

Row 3: Work as Row 2.

Break yarn and fasten off.

TO FINISH

Weave any loose yarn ends into the back of your work so they are not visible from the right side.

Lightly steam all the garment pieces.

Using matching sewing thread, position the zip between the Front and Back panels and sew securely in place.

Using cotton yarn, with Front and Back panels wrong side together, sew all round the outside of the bag, catching in the two ends of the handle at one end of the zip.

colourway a

+CROPPED TEE

YOU WILL NEED

YARN

For shorter version

3(3:3:3:4:4) x 113g (4oz) hanks of Jill Draper Makes Stuff *Hudson 100% Superwash Merino*, or a similar aran-weight wool yarn, in bright yellow (Daffodil)

For longer version

3(3:4:4:4:5) x 113g (4oz) hanks of Jill Draper Makes Stuff *Hudson 100% Superwash Merino*, or a similar aran-weight wool yarn, in bright yellow (Daffodil)

CROCHET HOOK

5mm (US size H/8) crochet hook

OTHER EQUIPMENT

Blunt-ended needle or tapestry needle for weaving in yarn ends and seaming

TENSION

15 sts and 10 rows to 10cm (4in) measured over treble crochet using a 5mm (US size H/8) crochet hook

ABBREVIATIONS

See page 9

SIZE (UK)	6	8	10	12	14	16
To fit bust (cm)	76	81	86	91	97	102
To fit bust (in)	30	32	34	36	38	40
Actual bust (cm)	80	85	90	95	101	106
Actual bust (in)	31½	33½	35½	37½	39¾	41¾
Length (cm) – shorter version	39	39	40	41	42	43
Length (in) – shorter version	15¼	15¼	15¾	16 1/8	16½	16 7/8
Length (cm) – longer version	46	46	47	48	49	50
Length (in) – longer version	18	18	18½	19	19¼	19½
Sleeve seam (cm)	1.5	1.5	2	2	3	3
Sleeve seam (in)	½	½	¾	¾	1¼	1¼

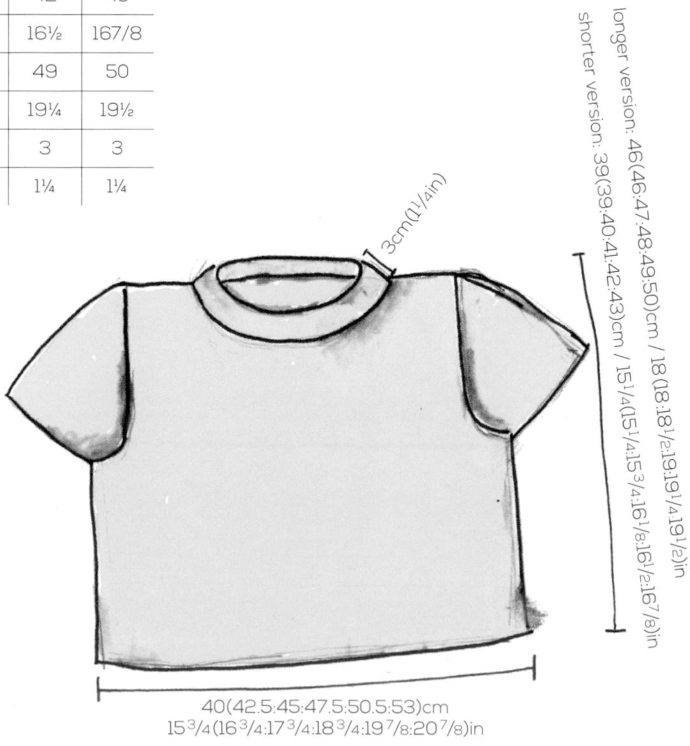

3cm(1¼in)

longer version: 46(46:47:48:49:50)cm / 18(18:18½:19:19¼:19½)in
shorter version: 39(39:40:41:42:43)cm / 15¼(15¼:15¾:16⅛:16½:16⅞)in

40(42.5:45:47.5:50.5:53)cm
15¾(16¾:17¾:18¾:19⅞:20⅞)in

FRONT

Foundation row: Using a 5mm (US size H/8) crochet hook, make 58(62:66:70:74:78) chain + 3 chain.
Cont working in rows, turning at end of each row.
Row 1: 1 tr in third ch from hook, 1 tr in each ch to end of row.
Row 2: 3 ch (counts as first tr), 1 tr in each st to end of row, ending with 1 tr in third of 3-ch of prev row. *(60(64:68:72:76:80) sts)*
Row 3: Work as Row 2.
Row 4: Work as Row 2.
Cont in this tr patt as set until work measures 21(21:22:23:24:25)cm/8¼(8¼:8½:9:9½:9¾)in for the shorter version and 29(29:30:31:32:33)cm/11½(11½:11¾:12¼:12½:13)in for the longer version, ending with a WS row.
SHAPE ARMHOLE
Row 1: 1 ch, sl st in next 2(3:3:4:4:4) sts, 3 ch, miss 1 st, 1 tr in each st to last 5(6:6:7:7:7) sts, miss 1 st, 1 tr in next st, turn. *(52(54:58:60:64:68) sts)*
Row 2: 3 ch, miss 1 st, 1 tr in each st to last 2 sts, miss 1 st, 1 tr in last st, turn. *(50(52:56:58:62:66) sts)*
Row 3: Work as Row 2. *(48(50:54:56:60:64) sts)* * * *
Cont working without shaping until work measures 32(32:33:34:35:36)cm/12½(12½:13:13¼:13¾:14¼)in for the shorter version and 40(40:41:42:43:44)cm/15¾(15¾:16¼:16½:17:17¼)in for the longer version, ending with a WS row.

SHAPE NECK

Row 1: 3 ch (counts as first tr), 1 tr in each of next 12(13:14:15:16:17) sts, miss 1 st, work a dc dec (2dctog) over 2 sts, sl st 16(16:18:18:20:22) sts, dc2tog over 2 sts, miss 1 st, 1 tr in each of next 13(14:15:16:17:18) sts.
Work in short rows as folls:

Row 2: 3 ch (counts as first tr), 1 tr in each of next 12(13:14:15:16:17) sts, miss 1 st, 1 tr in next st, turn. *(14(15:16:17:18:19) sts)*

Row 3: 3 ch (counts as first tr), miss 1 st, 1 tr in each st to end of row, turn. *(13(14:15:16:17:18) sts)*

Row 4: 3 ch (counts as first tr), 1 tr in each of next 10(11:12:13:14:15) sts, miss 1 st, 1 tr in next st, turn. *(12(13:14:15:16:17) sts)*

Row 5: 3 ch (counts as first tr), miss 1 st, 1 tr in each st to end of row. *(11(12:13:14:15:16) sts)*

Row 6: 3 ch (counts as first tr), 1 tr in each st to end of row.

Row 7: 3 ch (counts as first tr), 1 tr in each st to end of row.
Break yarn and fasten off.
With WS facing, rejoin yarn to other side of neck, 15(16:17:18:19:20) sts from shoulder edge.

Row 1: 3 ch (counts as first tr), miss 1 st, 1 tr in each st to end of row. *(14(15:16:17:18:19) sts)*

Row 2: 3 ch (counts as first tr), 1 tr in each of next 11(12:13:14:15:16) sts, miss 1 st, 1 tr in next st, turn. *(13(14:15:16:17:18) sts)*

Row 3: 3 ch (counts as first tr), miss 1 st, 1 tr in each st to end of row. *(12(13:14:15:16:17) sts)*

Row 4: 3 ch (counts as first tr), 1 tr in each st to last 2 sts before neck edge, miss 1 st, 1 tr in next st, turn. *(11(12:13:14:15:16) sts)*

Row 5: 3 ch (counts as first tr), 1 tr in each st to end of row.

Row 6: 3 ch (counts as first tr), 1 tr in each st to end of row.
Break yarn and fasten off.

BACK

Work as given for Front until ***.
Cont working without shaping until work measures 39(39:40:41:42:43)cm/15¼(15¼:15¾:16¼:16½:17)in for the shorter version and 47(47:48:49:50:51)cm/18½(18½:18¾:19¼:19¾:20)in for the longer version, ending with a WS row.

Next row (RS): 3 ch (counts as first tr), 1 tr in each of next 10(11:12:13:14:15) sts.
Break yarn and fasten off.
With RS facing, rejoin yarn to other side of neck, 11(12:13:14:15:16) sts from end of row, 3 ch (counts as first tr), 1 tr in each st to end of row.
Break yarn and fasten off.

SLEEVES (MAKE 2)

Foundation row: Using a 5mm (US size H/8) crochet hook, make 43(44:45:47:49:50) chain + 3 chain.
Cont working in rows, turning at end of each row, work from top of Sleeve down as folls:

Row 1: 1 tr in fourth ch from hook, 1 tr in each st to end of row.

Row 2: 3 ch (counts as first tr), 1 tr in each st to end of row. *(44(45:46:48:50:51) sts)*

Row 3: Sl st in 6(6:7:7:8:9) sts, 3 ch (counts as first tr), miss 1 st, 1 tr in next st, 1 tr to last 9(9:10:10:11:12) sts, miss 1 st, 1 tr in each of next 2 sts, turn. *(30(31:30:32:32:31) sts)*

Row 4: 3 ch (counts as first tr), miss 1 st, 1 tr in next st, 1 tr in each st to last 3 sts, miss 1 st, 1 tr in each of next 2 sts. *(28(29:28:30:30:29) sts)*
Rep Row 4 a further 9 times. *(10(11:10:12:12:11) sts)*
Break yarn and fasten off.

TO FINISH

Weave any loose yarn ends into the back of your work so they are not visible from the right side.
Lightly steam all the garment pieces.
Seam together the Back and Fronts at the shoulders.
Pin the sleeveheads into the armhole openings before sewing them in place.
Sew the Back and Fronts together along the side seams, stitching from the bottom edge of the garment up to the underarm, then down along the underarm Sleeve seams to the cuffs.

ADD NECK EDGING

With RS facing, rejoin yarn at back of garment as folls:

Next round: 3 ch, 1 tr all way round neckline, join rnd with a sl st in top of 3-ch.

Next round: 3 ch (counts as first tr), 1 tr in each st to end, join rnd with a sl st in top of 3-ch.
Rep last round once more.
Break yarn and fasten off.

denim plaid scarf

DENIM PLAID SCARF

YOU WILL NEED

YARN

A 7 x 50g (1¾oz) balls of Rowan *Original Denim*, or a similar double-knitting-weight denim cotton yarn, in pale blue (1 Memphis)
B 3 x 50g (1¾oz) balls of Rowan *Handknit Cotton DK*, or a similar double-knitting-weight cotton yarn, in ecru (251 Ecru)

CROCHET HOOK
4mm (US size G/6) crochet hook

OTHER EQUIPMENT
Blunt-ended needle or tapestry needle for weaving in yarn ends and seaming

TENSION
22 sts and 12 rows to 10cm (4in) measured over treble crochet using a 4mm (US size G/6) crochet hook

ABBREVIATIONS
See page 9

128cm (50 ³/₈in)
35cm (13 ³/₄in)

SCARF

Using Col B, prepare three intarsia bobbins B for the verticals in this plaid patt (see opposite).
Foundation row: Using a 4mm (G/6) crochet hook and Col A, make 77 chain + 2 chain.
Cont working in rows, turning at end of each row.
Next row (RS): 1 tr in third ch from hook (counts as first tr), 1 tr in each ch to end of row. *(77 sts)*
Work from chart as folls:
Row 1 (WS): Using Col A, 3 ch (does NOT count as first tr), 1 tr in st at base of ch, 1 tr in each of next 10 sts; *using one Col B intarsia bobbin, 1 tr in each of next 5 sts; using Col A, 1 tr in each of next 20 sts; rep from * to last 16 sts; using final Col B intarsia bobbin, 1 tr in each of next 5 sts; using Col A, 1 tr in each of next 11 sts.
Rep last row a further 5 times, using Col B intarsia bobbins as required.
Break off Col A.

Row 7: Using Col B only, 3 ch (does NOT count as first tr), 1 tr in st at base of ch, 1 tr in each st to end of row.
Rep last row a further 2 times.
Rows 10–15: Rep Row 1 a further 6 times.
Rows 1–15 form the 15-row rep.
Work the 15-row rep a total of 11 times.
Note the second rep Row 1 will be a RS row and the side on which the rep starts will alt.
Once the patt reps have been completed, work the final row as folls:
Next row: Using Col A only, 3 ch (does NOT count as first st), 1 tr in st at base of ch, 1 tr in each st to end of row.
Break yarn and fasten off.

TO FINISH

Weave any loose yarn ends into the back of your work so they are not visible from the right side.

⁺INTARSIA

MAKING AN INTARSIA BOBBIN

STEP 1 Make an intarsia bobbin for each vertical stripe to stop the yarn from tangling. Lie the yarn across your palm, wrap it around your index finger with the tail of the yarn at the bottom.

STEP 2 With the working yarn, wrap in a figure of eight around your thumb and index finger.

STEP 3 Cont to work in this figure of eight until you have built up a good amount of yarn or enough to crochet the vertical that this bobbin is for.

STEP 4 Slip the yarn from your fingers by pinching the centre of your figure of eight. Snip the yarn end and wrap tightly around the centre of your bobbin.

CROCHETING IN INTARSIA

STEP 5 Fasten the working yarn by slipping the end under some of the wraps you've just made to secure your bobbin. If you pull gently, the yarn feeds easily from this point.

STEP 1 Crocheting using the intarsia technique is really simple once you have all your bobbins made. Crochet up to the last yrh of the last st before your colour change.

STEP 2 Simply pass the coloured bobbin you are currently working with over the bobbin you are about to start crocheting with.

STEP 3 Work the final yrh with your new colour, trapping your old bobbin into place, securing the colour change. Cont working with your new bobbin until you change colour.

POMPOM BERET

//

YOU WILL NEED

YARN
2 x 100g (3½oz) hanks of Misti Alpaca *Chunky*, or a similar chunky-weight wool yarn, in lilac (1742 California Lilac)

CROCHET HOOK
7mm (US size K/10½) crochet hook

OTHER EQUIPMENT
Blunt-ended needle or tapestry needle for weaving in yarn ends and seaming

TENSION
15 sts and 15 rounds to 10cm (4in) measured over double crochet using a 7mm (US size K/10½) crochet hook

ABBREVIATIONS
See page 9

//

BERET

Foundation ring: Using a 7mm (US size K/10½) crochet hook, make a 4 chain, join with a sl st in first ch to make a ring.

Cont working in rnds, with RS always facing.

Round 1: 1 ch, [1 dc] 5 times in centre of ring, join with a sl st in top of 1-ch.

Round 2: 1 ch (counts as first dc), 1 dc in base of same st to make first inc, 2 dc in each st to end of rnd, join with a sl st in top of 1-ch. *(12 sts)*

Round 3: 1 ch (counts as first dc), 2 dc in next st, *1 dc in next st, 2 dc in second st; rep from * to end of rnd, join with a sl st in top of 1-ch. *(18 sts)*

Round 4: 1 ch (counts as first dc), 1 dc in next st, 2 dc in foll st, *1 dc in each of next 2 sts, 2 dc in third st; rep from * to end of rnd, join with a sl st in top of 1-ch. *(24 sts)*

Round 5: 1 ch (counts as first dc), 1 dc in each of next 2 sts, 2 dc in foll st, *1 dc in each of next 3 sts, 2 dc in fourth st; rep from * to end of rnd, join with a sl st in top of 1-ch. *(30 sts)*

Cont working in patt as set, inc the number of single dc sts between each inc st by 1 st each rnd, until you have 108 sts in a rnd.

Next round: 1 ch (counts as first dc), 1 dc in each st of rnd, join with a sl st in top of 1-ch.

Rep last rnd a further 7 times.

Round 1: 1 ch (counts as first dc), 1 dc in each of next 15 sts, dc2tog (a dec st worked across 2 sts), *1 dc in each of next 16 sts, dc2tog; rep from * to end of rnd, join with a sl st in top of 1-ch. *(102 sts)*

Round 2: 1 ch (counts as first dc), 1 dc in each of next 14 sts, dc2tog, *1 dc in each of next 15 sts, dc2tog; rep from * to end of rnd, join with a sl st in top of 1-ch. *(96 sts)*

Round 3: 1 ch (counts as first dc), 1 dc in each of next 13 sts, dc2tog, *1 dc in each of next 14 sts, dc2tog; rep from * to end of rnd, join with a sl st in top of 1-ch. *(90 sts)*

Cont working in patt as set, dec the number of single dc sts between each dec st by 1 st each rnd, until 54 sts rem in a rnd.

Final round: 1 ch, 1 dc in each st, join with a sl st in top of 1-ch.

Break yarn and fasten off.

TO FINISH

Weave any loose yarn ends into the back of your work so they are not visible from the right side.

Use any remaining yarn to make a large pompom for the top of the beret. If you only have a small amount of the main colour yarn left over, use a contrast colour yarn or a mix of the main colour with a contrast colour yarn.

pompom beret

⁺ZIGZAG SHOPPER

SIZE: **32 x 30 x 12cm**
(12½ x 11¾ x 4¾in)

YOU WILL NEED

YARN
4 x 100g (3½oz) balls of Prick Your Finger *Carpet Yarn*, or a similar aran-weight yarn, in natural

OTHER MATERIAL
Lining fabric

CROCHET HOOK
5mm (US size H/8) crochet hook

OTHER EQUIPMENT
Blunt-ended needle or tapestry needle for weaving in yarn ends and seaming

TENSION
Achieving an exact tension is not vital when crocheting this bag, as the finished size of the shopper can vary

ABBREVIATIONS
See page 9

SPECIAL ABBREVIATIONS
single ttr group = work 3 triple treble in next double crochet until one loop of each remains on hook, yarn over and draw through all four loops
double ttr group = work 3 triple treble in same double crochet as last group until one loop of each remains on hook (four loops on hook), miss 5 double crochet, in next double crochet work 3 triple treble until one loop of each remains on hook, yarn over and draw through all seven loops on hook

DESIGN NOTE
This bag is made up of four separate panels of different yet simple crochet stitches, which are sewn together with a fabric lining.

Special abbreviations

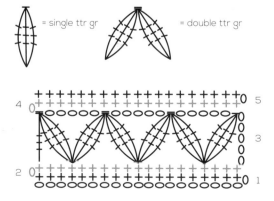

BAG BASE

Foundation row: Using a 5mm (US size H/8) crochet hook, make 42 chain + 2 chain.

Cont working in rows, turning at end of each row.

Row 1 (RS): 1 tr in third ch from hook (does NOT count as first tr), 1 tr in each ch to end of row. *(42 sts)*

Row 2: 3 ch (does NOT count as first tr), 1 tr in each st to end of row (do not work last st of row in top of tch).

Rep Row 2 until work measures approx 14cm (5½in). Break yarn and fasten off.

FRONT AND BACK PANELS (MAKE 2)

These treble crochet panels form the Front and Back of the bag.

Foundation row: Using a 5mm (US size H/8) crochet hook, make 33 chain + 2 chain.

Row 1 (RS): 1 tr in third ch from hook (does NOT count as first tr), 1 tr in each ch to end. *(33 sts)*

Row 2: 3 ch, 1 tr in each ch to end of row, ending with 1 tr in top of tch.

Rep Row 2 until work measures approx 32cm (12½in). Break yarn and fasten off.

SIDE PANELS (MAKE 2)

These zigzag stitch panels form the narrow side end panels of the bag.

Using a 5mm (US size H/8) crochet hook, make 30 chain + 2 chain.

Row 1 (RS): 1 dc in second ch from hook, 1 dc in each ch to end of row, turn. *(29 sts)*

Row 2: 1 ch, 1 dc in each dc to end of row, turn.

Row 3: 5 ch (counts as first triple treble (ttr)), miss next 3 sts, work 1 single ttr group in next dc, *1 double ttr group,

5 ch; rep from * to last 3 dc, in same dc as last group work 3 ttr until one loop of each rems on hook (4 loops), 1 ttr in last dc until 5 loops rem on hook, yo and draw through all 5 loops, turn.

Row 4: 1 ch, 1 dc in top of first group, 5 dc in 5-ch space, *1 dc in top of next group, 5 dc in next 5-ch space; rep from * to last group, 1 dc in fifth of 5-ch at beg of previous row, turn.

Row 5: 1 ch, 1 dc in each dc to end of row, turn.

Rows 2–5 form the zigzag stitch pattern.

Cont in this zigzag stitch pattern until work measures approx 32cm (12½in), ending with a Row 2. Break yarn and fasten off.

STRAPS (MAKE 2)

Using a 5mm (US size H/8) crochet hook, make 6 chain + 2 chain.

Row 1: 1 tr in third ch from hook (counts as first tr), 1 tr in each ch to end of row, turn.

Row 2: 3 ch, 1 tr in each st to end of row, turn.

Rep Row 2 until Strap measures approx 50cm (19½in) or preferred length. (Bear in mind that the bag straps will stretch through usage, so it is a good idea to make them slightly shorter.)

Break yarn and fasten off.

TO FINISH

Weave any loose yarn ends into the back of your work so they are not visible from the right side.

Lightly steam all the panels to ensure they sit flat.

To make the lining, draw around the panels, leaving a 1.5cm seam allowance. Stitched all the lining pieces together. Handstitch the bag panels together and then catch in the lining around the top of the bag.

GRANNY STRIPE CHUNKY SWEATER

//

YOU WILL NEED

YARN

4 x 100g (3½oz) hanks of Quince & Co *Osprey*, or a
similar aran-weight wool yarn, in one colour:
A dark blue (Peacoat)
1 x 100g (3½oz) hanks of Quince & Co *Osprey*, or a
similar aran-weight wool yarn, in each of five colours:
B dark pink (Rosa Rugosa)
C mustard (Honey)
D dark red (Malbec)
E pale grey (Chanterelle)
F pale blue (Lupine)

CROCHET HOOK

6.5mm (US size K/10½) crochet hook

OTHER EQUIPMENT

Blunt-ended needle or tapestry needle for weaving in yarn
ends and seaming

For the clutch bag

25cm (10in) zip
Lining fabric

TENSION

4 clusters of 3 treble crochet sts and 8 rows to 10cm (4in)
measured over granny stripe stitch pattern using a 6.5mm
(US size K/10½) crochet hook

ABBREVIATIONS

See page 9

SIZE (UK)	8	10	12	14	16
To fit bust (cm)	81	86	91	97	102
To fit bust (in)	32	34	36	38	40
Actual bust (cm)	108	113	118	123	128
Actual bust (in)	42½	44½	46½	48½	50½
Length (cm)	50	50	51	52	53
Length (in)	19½	19½	20	20½	20¾
Sleeve seam (cm)	46	46	46	48	48
Sleeve seam (in)	18	18	18	19	19

46(46:46:48:48)cm
18(18:18:19:19)in

54(56.5:59:61.5:64)cm
21¼(22¼:23¼:24¼:25¼)in

50(50:51:52:53)cm
19½(19½:20:20½:20¾)in

granny stripe chunky sweater

BACK

Foundation row: Using a 6.5mm (US size K/10½) crochet hook and Col A, make 61(64:67:70:73) chain + 3 chain.

Cont working in rows, turning at end of each row.

Row 1: 1 tr in fourth ch from hook, miss 2 ch, *3 tr in next ch, miss 2 sts; rep from * to last st, 2 tr in last ch, turn.

Row 2: 3 ch, miss 2 sts, 3 tr in first space, *miss 3 sts, 3 tr in next space; rep from * to end of row, 1 tr in top of 3-ch from previous row, turn.

Change to Col B.

Row 3: 3 ch, 1 tr in first space, *miss 3 sts, 3 tr in next space; rep from * to end of row, ending with miss 3 sts, 2 tr in top of 3-ch of previous row, turn.

Change to Col C.

Row 4: Work as Row 2.

Change to Col D.

Row 5: Work as Row 3.

Change to Col E.

Row 6: Work as Row 2.

Change to Col F.

Row 7: Work as Row 3.

Rows 2–7 form the granny stripe stitch pattern. Cont working in this granny stripe stitch pattern until work measures 50(50:51:52:53)cm/ (20(20:20½:20¾:21½)in).

Break yarn and fasten off.

FRONT

Foundation row: Using a 6.5mm (US size K/10½) crochet hook and Col A, make 61(64:67:70:73) chain + 3 chain.

Cont working in rows, turning at end of each row.

Work as for Back until work measures 42(42:43:44:45) cm/16½(16½:17:17¼:17¾)in, ending with a RS row.

SHAPE NECK

Work each side of neck separately.

Sizes 8, 12 and 16

With WS facing, changing colours as set in granny stripe stitch pattern, work righthand side of neck as folls:

Row 1: 3 ch, 3 tr in first space and foll 7(–:8:–:9) spaces, miss 2 sts, 1 tr in next st, turn.

Row 2: 3 ch, 3 tr in first space and foll 6(–:7:–:8) spaces, 2 tr in top of 3-ch.

Row 3: 3 ch, 3 tr in first space and foll 6(–:7:–:8) spaces, 1 tr in top of 3-ch.

Rows 4–7: Cont working straight in granny stripe stitch pattern without shaping.

Break yarn and fasten off.

With WS facing, rejoin yarn to lefthand side of neck and cont working as folls:

Row 1: Leave a gap of 9 sts at centre, 3 ch, 3 tr in next space and foll 7(–:8:–:9) spaces, 1 tr in top of 3-ch.

Row 2: 3 ch, 1 tr in first space, 3 tr in next 7(–:8:–:9) spaces, 1 tr in top of 3-ch.

Row 3: 3 ch, miss first space, 3 tr in next 7(–:8:–:9) spaces, 1 tr in top of 3-ch.

Rows 4–7: Cont working straight in granny stripe stitch

pattern without shaping.
Break yarn and fasten off.

Sizes 10 and 14
With WS facing, changing colours as set in granny stripe stitch pattern, work righthand side of neck as folls:
Row 1: 3 ch, 3 tr in first space and foll –(7:–:8:–) spaces, 2 tr in next space, turn.
Row 2: 3 ch, 1 tr in first space and foll –(7:–:8:–) spaces, 2 tr in top of 3-ch, turn.
Row 3: 3 ch, 3 tr in next space and foll –(6:–:7:–) spaces, 1 tr in next space, 1 tr in top of 3-ch.
Rows 4–7: Cont working straight in granny stripe stitch pattern without shaping.
Break yarn and fasten off.
With WS facing, rejoin yarn to lefthand side of neck and cont working as folls:
Row 1: Leaving a gap of 9 sts at centre, 3 ch, 1 tr in same space and 3 tr in foll –(8:–:9:–) spaces, 1 tr in top of 3-ch.
Row 2: 3 ch, 1 tr in space, 3 tr in foll –(7:–:8:–) spaces, 1 tr in next space, 1 tr in top of 3-ch.
Row 3: 3 ch, 1 tr in space, 3 tr in foll –(7:–8:–) spaces, 1 tr in top of 3-ch.
Rows 4–7: Cont working straight in granny stripe stitch pattern without shaping.
Break yarn and fasten off.

SLEEVES (MAKE 2)
Foundation row: Using a 6.5mm (US size K/10½) crochet hook and Col A, make 28(28:28:34:34) chain + 3 chain.
Cont working in rows, turning at end of each row.
Row 1: 1 tr in fourth ch from hook (counts as first tr), miss 2 ch, *3 tr in next ch, miss 2 ch; rep from * to last st, 2 tr in last ch, turn.

Row 2: 3 ch, 3 tr in each space to end of row, work 1 tr in top of 3-ch from previous row, turn.
Row 3: 3 ch, 1 tr in first space, *3 tr in next space; rep from * to end of row, ending with 2 tr in top of 3-ch, turn.
Rows 2–3 form the stitch pattern.
Cont working in stitch pattern as set for 38(38:38:40:40) rows, but working inc rows on the 5th, 12th, 17th, 24th and 29th rows as folls:
Inc row: 3 ch, 3 tr in next space and all spaces to end of row, 1 tr in top of 3-ch.
The inc rows alter the stitch pattern at the beg and ends of each row, so after an inc row your next row will be Row 3. Cont in stitch pattern from here until next inc row.
Break yarn and fasten off.

TO FINISH
Weave any loose yarn ends into the back of your work so they are not visible from the right side.
Lightly steam all the garment pieces.
Seam together the Back and Fronts at the shoulders.
Pin the centre of the sleeveheads to the shoulder seams and stitch in place.
Sew the Back and Fronts together along the side seams, stitching from the bottom edge of the garment up to the underarm, then down along the underarm Sleeve seams to the cuffs.

ADD NECKBAND
Round 1: With a 6.5mm US size K/10½) crochet hook and Col A, rejoin the yarn at the back of the garment with a 3 ch, 2 tr in same space as 3-ch and work in groups of 3 tr all round neckline, join with a sl st to top of first 3-ch.
Round 2: Work as Round 1 but beg with a 3 ch and work 3 tr in spaces of previous rnd, join with a sl st.
Break yarn and fasten off. Weave in any loose yarn ends.

CLUTCH BAG TO MATCH

CLUTCH BAG OUTERS (MAKE 2)

Foundation row: Using a 6.5mm (US size K/10½) crochet hook and Col A, make 28 chain + 3 chain.

Row 1: 1 tr in fourth ch from hook, miss 2 ch, *3 tr in next ch, miss 2 ch; rep from * to last st, 2 tr in last ch, turn.

Row 2: 3 ch, miss 2 sts, 3 tr in first space, *miss 3 sts, 3 tr in next space, rep from * to end of row, work 1 tr in top of 3-ch from previous row, turn.
Change to Col B.

Row 3: 3 ch, 1 tr in first space, *miss 3 sts, 3 tr in next space, rep from * to end of row, ending with miss 3 sts, 2 tr in top of 3-ch, turn.
Cont working in rows, turning at end of each row.
Change to Col C.

Row 4: Work as Row 2.
Change to Col D.

Row 5: Work as Row 3.
Change to Col E.

Row 6: Work as Row 2.
Change to Col F.

Row 7: Work as Row 3.
Rows 2–7 form the granny stripe stitch pattern.
Cont working in this granny stripe stitch pattern until work measures approx 18.5cm (7¼in).
Break yarn and fasten off.

HANDLE

Foundation row: Using a 6.5mm (US size K/10½) crochet hook and Col A, make 40 chain + 3 chain.

Row 1: 1 tr in fourth ch from hook, 1 tr in each ch to end of row.
Break yarn and fasten off.

TO FINISH

Using a sewing machine, stitch together the lining fabric and zip to make the bag lining.
Handstitch together the clutch bag outer pieces, leaving the top edge open and catching in both ends of the handle together at one end.
Catch in the lining so all the raw edges are hidden and the zip sits neatly at the opening of the bag.

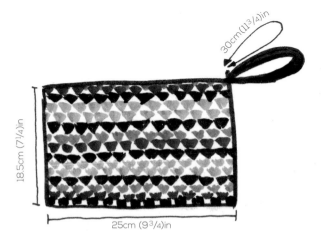

30cm(11¾)in

18.5cm (7¼)in

25cm (9¾)in

poodle slippers

POODLE SLIPPERS

YOU WILL NEED

YARN
2 x 50g (1¾oz) balls of Rowan *Pure Wool 4ply*, or a similar 4ply-weight wool yarn, in pale pink (468 Shell)
2 x 25g (⅞oz) balls of Rowan *Mohair Haze*, or a similar 4ply-weight mohair yarn, in pale pink (521 Baby)

OTHER MATERIALS
Small amount of black embroidery thread or yarn, for adding the facial features
30cm (12in) square pink suede or a similar non-slip fabric, for soles of slippers

CROCHET HOOKS
4mm and 4.5mm (US size G/6 and 7) crochet hooks

OTHER EQUIPMENT
Blunt-ended needle or tapestry needle for weaving in yarn ends and seaming

TENSION
18 sts and 20 rows to 10cm (4in) measured over double crochet loop stitch using a 4mm (US size G/6) crochet hoo

ABBREVIATIONS
See page 9

SPECIAL ABBREVIATIONS:
Double crochet loop stitch = see below for instructions.

DESIGN NOTE
The two yarns required for these slippers are worked together at the same time throughout.

DOUBLE CROCHET LOOP STITCH

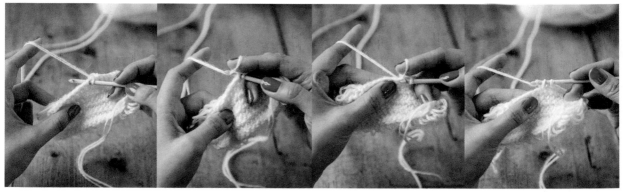

STEP 1 Loop stitch is simple to work and creates a really fun effect. It's worked on a WS row, so the loops will be seen from the right side. Work your stitch as normal as if to work a dc.

STEP 2 When working your yarn round hook, wrap the yarn around your index finger at the same time to create a loop.

STEP 3 Keeping the yarn wrapped around your finger, draw the yarn through as your normally would.

STEP 4 Finish the stitch by yrh and drawing through the rem two loops on your hook. Remove your finger from the loop and move onto the next stitch. Once you've finished your work, tighten up your stitches by simply gently pulling the loops from the right side of your work.

SNOUTS (MAKE 2)

Foundation row: Using a 4mm (US size G/6) crochet hook and two strands of yarn, make 8 chain + 1 chain. Cont working in rows, turning at end of each row.
Row 1: 1 dc in second ch from hook, 1 dc in each ch to end of row. *(8 sts)*
Row 2: 1 ch (counts as first dc), 1 double crochet loop stitch in each st to end of row.
Row 3: 1 ch (counts as first dc), 1 dc in base of ch st, 1 dc in each st to last st of row, 2 dc in final st. *(10 sts)*
Row 4: Work as Row 2.
Rows 5–20: Rep Rows 3–4 a further 8 times. *(26 sts)*
Rows 21–28: Rep Rows 3–4 a further 4 times but when working central 8 sts in double crochet loop stitch wrap yarn twice round forefinger instead of once to make loops longer for shaggy hair. *(34 sts)*
Row 29: 1 ch, 1 dc in each st to end of row.
Break yarn and fasten off.

BACKS (MAKE 2)

Foundation row: Using a 4mm (US size G/6) crochet hook and two strands of yarn, make 30 chain + 1 chain. Cont working in rows, turning at end of each row.
Row 1: 1 dc in second ch from hook, 1 dc in each ch to end of row. *(30 sts)*
Row 2: 1 ch (counts as first dc), 1 double crochet loop stitch in each st to end of row.
Row 3: 1 ch (counts as first dc), 1 dc in each st to end of row.

Rows 4–13: Rep Rows 2–3 a further 5 times.
Row 14: Work as Row 3.
Break yarn and fasten off.

EARS (MAKE 4)

Foundation row: Using a 4.5mm (US size 7) crochet hook and two strands of yarn, make 10 chain + 3 chain. Cont working in rows, turning at end of each row.
Row 1: 1 tr in fourth ch from hook (counts as first tr), 1 tr in each st to end of the row. *(11 sts)*
Row 2: 3 ch (counts as first tr), 1 tr in each st to end of row.
Rows 3–4: Work as Row 2 a further 2 times.
Row 5: 3 ch, [2trtog over 2 sts] 5 times. *(6 sts)*
Break yarn and fasten off.

TO FINISH

Weave any loose yarn ends into the back of your work so they are not visible from the right side.
Lightly steam all the slipper pieces.
Stitch the thinner ends of the Backs to the tops of the Snouts, creating the openings for your feet.
Draw roughly around your feet onto the piece of suede, creating shapes for the soles of the slippers. Cut these pieces out and pin them in place around the slipper bases before sewing.
Pin the Ears in place on either side of the longer loops on the Snouts and securely sew.
Using black embroidery thread, add two eyes and a nose to each slipper in satin stitch.

+TWEED CARDI

//

YOU WILL NEED

YARN
8(8:8:8:9) x 100g (3½oz) balls of Rico *Fashion Colour Touch*, or a similar super-chunky-weight wool yarn, in multi colours (004 Yellow Mix)

OTHER MATERIALS
Five 2.5cm (1in) diameter buttons

CROCHET HOOK
9mm (US size N/13) crochet hook

OTHER EQUIPMENT
Blunt-ended needle or tapestry needle for weaving in yarn ends and seaming

TENSION
9½ sts and 8 rows to 10cm (4in) measured over half treble pattern using a 9mm (US size N/13) crochet hook

ABBREVIATIONS
See page 9

SIZE (UK)	8	10	12	14	16
To fit bust (cm)	81	86	91	97	102
To fit bust (in)	32	34	36	38	40
Actual bust (cm)	84	89	94	100	105
Actual bust (in)	33	35	37	39½	41½
Length (cm)	49	49	49	49	49
Length (in)	19¼	19¼	19¼	19¼	19¼
Sleeve seam (cm)	36	36	36	36	36
Sleeve seam (in)	14	14	14	14	14

36cm (14in)

49cm (19¼in)

32(34.5:37:40:42.5)cm
12⅝(13⅝:14⅝:15¾:16¾)in

BACK

Begin by working the rib, which is crocheted horizontally across body.

Using a 9mm (US size N/13) crochet hook, make 8 chain + 1 chain.

Cont working in rows, turning at end of each row.

Row 1: 1 dc in second ch from hook, 1 dc in each ch to end of row. *(8 sts)*

Row 2: 1 ch, sl st in each of next 8 sts.

Row 3: 1 ch (counts as first dc), 1 dc in each of next 7 sts.

Rep Rows 2–3 a further 21(23:25:27:29) times.

With RS facing, turn rib on its side and work 1 dc 29(31:33:36:38) times across longest edge.

Row 1 (WS): 2 ch (counts as first htr), 1 htr in each st to end of row.

This row forms the htr patt.

Rows 2–3: 2 ch (counts as first htr), 1 htr in each st to end of row.

Row 4: 2 ch, 2 htr in next st, 1 htr in each st to last 2 sts, 2 htr in next st, 1 htr in top of tch. *(31(33:35:38:40) sts)*

Rows 5–9: 2 ch (counts as first htr), 1 htr in each st to end of row.

Row 10: Work as Row 4. *(33(35:37:40:42) sts)*

Rows 11–15: 2 ch (counts as first htr), 1 htr in each st to end of row.

Row 16: Work as Row 4. *(35(37:39:42:44) sts)*

Rows 17–18: 2 ch (counts as first htr), 1 htr in each st to end of row.

SHAPE ARMHOLE

Row 19: Sl st in each of next 4 sts, 2 ch (counts as first htr), htr2tog, 1 htr in each st to last 6 sts, htr2tog, 1 htr in next st, turn. *(27(29:31:34:36) sts)*

Row 20: 2 ch (counts as first htr), 1 htr in each st to end of row.

Row 21: 2 ch (counts as first htr), htr2tog, 1 htr in each st to last 3 sts, htr2tog, 1 htr in top of tch. *(25(27:29:32:34) sts)*

Rows 22–23: Work as Rows 20–21. *(23(25:27:30:32) sts)*

Rows 24–32: Work as Row 20.

SHAPE SHOULDER

Work each side separately.

Row 33 (WS): 2 ch (counts as 1 htr), 1 htr in each of next 5(6:7:8:9) sts, turn.

Row 34: 2 ch, 1 htr in next 2(3:3:4:4) sts.

Break yarn and fasten off.

With WS facing, rejoin yarn 6(7:8:9:10) sts from side edge.

Row 33 (WS): 2 ch (counts a 1 htr), 1 htr in each st to end of row, turn.

Row 34: Sl st in 3(3:4:4:5) sts, 2 ch, 1 htr in each of next 2(3:3:4:4) sts.

Break yarn and fasten off.

LEFT FRONT

Begin by working the rib, which is crocheted horizontally across body.

With a 9mm (US size N/13) crochet hook, make 8 chain + 1 chain.

Cont working in rows, turning at end of each row.

Row 1: 1 dc in second ch from hook, 1 dc in each ch to end of row.

Cont working in rows, turning at end of each row.

Row 2: 1 ch, sl st in each of next 8 sts.

Row 3: 1 ch (counts as first dc), 1 dc in each of next 7 sts.

Rep Rows 2–3 a further 11(12:13:14:15) times.

Break yarn and fasten off.

With RS facing, turn rib on its side and work 1 dc 15(16:17:18:19) times across longest edge.

Row 1 (WS): 2 ch (counts as first htr), 1 htr in each st to end of row.

This row forms the htr patt.

Rows 2–3: 2 ch (counts as first htr), 1 htr in each st to end of row.

Row 4: 2 ch (counts as first htr), 2 htr in next st, 1 htr in each st to end of row. *(16(17:18:19:20) sts)*

Rows 5–9: 2 ch (counts as first htr), 1 htr in each st to end of row.
Row 10: Work as Row 4. *(17(18:19:20:21) sts)*
Rows 11–15: 2 ch (counts as first htr), 1 htr in each st to end of row.
Row 16: Work as Row 4. *(18(19:20:21:22) sts)*
Rows 17–18: 2 ch (counts as first htr), 1 htr in each st to end of row.
SHAPE ARMHOLE
Row 19: 2 ch (counts as first htr), 1 htr in each st until 6 sts rem, htr2tog, 1 htr in next st, turn. *(14(15:16:17:18) sts)*
Row 20: 2 ch (counts as first htr), 1 htr in each st to end of row.
Row 21: 2 ch (counts as first htr), 1 htr in each st to last 3 sts, htr2tog, 1 htr in next st, turn. *(13(14:15:16:17) sts)*
Row 22: Work as Row 20.
Row 23: Work as Row 21. *(12(13:14:15:16) sts)*
Rows 24–28: Work as Row 20.
NECK SHAPING
Row 29: Sl st in each of next 3 sts, 2 ch, htr2tog, 1 htr in each st to end of row.
Row 30: 2 ch, 1 htr in each st to last 3 sts, htr2tog, 1 htr in next st.
Row 31: 2 ch, htr2tog, 1 htr in each st to end of row.
Row 32: Work as Row 30.
SHAPE SHOULDER
Row 33: 2 ch, 1 htr in next 5(6:7:8:9) sts, turn.
Row 34: Sl st in each of next 3(3:4:4:5) sts, 2 ch, 1 htr in each of next 2(3:3:4:4) sts.
Break yarn and fasten off.

RIGHT FRONT
Begin by working the rib, which is crocheted horizontally across body.
Using a 9mm (US size N/13) crochet hook, make 8 chain + 1 chain.
Cont working in rows, turning at end of each row.

Row 1: 1 dc in second ch from hook, 1 dc in each ch to end of row.
Row 2: 1 ch, sl st in each of next 8 sts.
Row 3: 1 ch (counts as first dc), 1 dc in each of next 7 sts.
Rep Rows 2–3 a further 10(11:12:13:14) times.
Cont to work buttonhole as folls:
Row 1: 1 ch, sl st in each of next 3 sts, 2 ch, miss 2 sts, sl st in each of next 3 sts.
Row 2: 1 ch (counts as first dc), 1 dc in each of next 7 sts.
Break yarn and fasten off.
With RS facing, turn rib on its side and work 1 dc 15(16:17:18:19) times across longest edge.
Row 1 (WS): 2 ch (counts as first htr), 1 htr in each st to end of row.
This row forms the htr patt.
Row 2: 2 ch (counts as first htr), 1 htr in each st to end of row.
Row 3: 2 ch (counts as first htr), 1 htr in each st until 2 sts rem, 1 ch, miss 1 st, 1 htr in last st.
Row 4: 2 ch (counts as first htr), 1 htr in each st to last 3 sts, htr2tog, 1 htr in next st. *(16(17:18:19:20) sts)*
Rows 5–8: 2 ch (counts as first htr), 1 htr in each st to end of row.
Row 9: Work as Row 3.
Row 10: Work as Row 4. *(17(18:19:20:21) sts)*
Rows 11–14: 2 ch (counts as first htr), 1 htr in each st to end of row.
Row 15: Work as Row 3.
Row 16: Work as Row 4. *(18(19:20:21:22) sts)*
Rows 17–18: 2 ch (counts as first htr), 1 htr in each st to end of row.
SHAPE ARMHOLE
Row 19: Sl st in each of next 4 sts, 2 ch (counts as first htr), htr2tog, 1 htr in each st to end of row. *(14(15:16:17:18) sts)*
Row 20: 2 ch, 1 htr in each st to end of row.
Row 21: 2 ch, htr2tog, 1 htr in each st to last 2 sts, 1 ch, miss 1 st, 1 htr in last st. *(13(14:15:16:17) sts)*

Row 22: Work as Row 20.
Row 23: Work as Row 21. *(12(13:14:15:16) sts)*
Rows 24–26: Work as Row 20.
Row 27: Work as Row 3.
Row 28: Work as Row 20.
SHAPE NECK
Row 29: 2 ch (counts as first htr), 1 htr in each st to last 6 sts, htr2tog, 1 htr in next st, turn.
Row 30: 2 ch (counts as first htr), htr2tog, 1 htr in each st to end of row.
Row 31: 2 ch (counts as first htr), 1 htr in each st to last 3 sts, htr2tog, 1 htr in next st, turn.
Row 32: Work as Row 30.
SHAPE SHOULDER
Row 33: 2 ch (counts as first 1htr), 1 htr in next 5(6:7:8:9) sts, turn.
Row 34: 2 ch, 1htr in next 2(3:3:4:4) sts.
Break yarn and fasten off.

SLEEVES (MAKES 2)
Begin by working the rib, which is crocheted horizontally around the wrist.
Using a 9mm (US size N/13) crochet hook, make 8 chain + 1 chain.
Cont working in rows, turning at end of each row.
Row 1: 1 dc in second ch from hook, 1 dc in each ch to end of row.
Cont working in rows, turning at end of each row.
Row 2: 1 ch, sl st in each of next 8 sts.
Row 3: 1 ch (counts as first dc), 1 dc in each of next 7 sts.
Rep Rows 2–3 a further 10(11:12:13:13) times.
Break yarn and fasten off.
With RS facing, turn rib on its side and work 1 dc 18(19:20:21:21) times across longest edge.

Row 1 (WS): 2 ch (counts as first htr), 1 htr in each st to end of row.
This row forms the htr patt.
Rows 2–3: 2 ch (counts as first htr), 1 htr in each st to end of row.
Row 4: 2 ch (counts as first htr), 2 htr in next st, 1 htr in each st to last 2 sts of row, 2 htr in next st and 1 htr in top of tch. *(20(21:22:23:23) sts)*
Rows 5–22: Work Rows 2–4 a further 6 times. *(32(33:34:35:35) sts)*
Row 24: Work as Rows 2–3.
SHAPE ARMHOLE
Row 25: Sl st in each of next 4 sts, 2 ch (counts as first htr), htr2tog, 1 htr in each st until 6 sts rem, htr2tog, 1 htr in next st, turn. *(24(25:26:27:27) sts)*
Row 26: 2 ch, htr2tog, 1 htr in each st to last 2 sts, htr2tog, turn. *(22(23:24:25:25) sts)*
Rep Row 26 a further 10 times. *(2(3:4:5:5) sts)*
Break yarn and fasten off.

TO FINISH
Weave any loose yarn ends into the back of your work so they are not visible from the right side.
Lightly steam all the garment pieces.
Seam together the Back and Fronts at the shoulders.
Pin the sleeveheads into the armhole openings before sewing them in place.
Sew the Back and Fronts together along the side seams, stitching from the bottom rib edge of the garment up to the underarm, then down along the underarm Sleeve seams to the rib cuffs.
Sew buttons on the Left Front to correspond with the buttonholes on the Right Front.

LOVE TO
CROCHET

GRANNY SQUARE COTTON TEE

YOU WILL NEED

YARN

Rico *Essentials Cotton DK*, or a similar double-knitting-weight cotton yarn, in three colours:
A 10 x 50g (1¾oz) balls in white (80 White)
B 6 x 50g (1¾oz) balls in blue (34 Medium Blue)
C 2 x 50g (1¾oz) balls in orange (87 Pumpkin)

CROCHET HOOK

4mm (US size G/6) crochet hook

OTHER EQUIPMENT

Blunt-ended needle or tapestry needle for weaving in yarn ends and seaming

TENSION

One Meadow Square once finished and blocked measures 8cm (3⅛in) square

ABBREVIATIONS

See page 9

DESIGN NOTE

This top is simple to make but takes a fair bit of sewing together once you've completed all your Meadow Squares. You need to make a total of 90 squares – 35 squares each for the Front and Back, then 10 squares for both Sleeves.

MEADOW SQUARE (MAKE 90)

Foundation ring: Using a 4mm (US size G/6) crochet hook and Col B, make 4 chain and join with a sl st in first ch to make ring. Cont working in rnds, with RS always facing.
Round 1: 5 ch (counts as 1 tr and 2 ch), *1 tr in centre of ring, 2 ch; rep from * a further 5 times, join with a sl st in third ch of 5-ch.

Round 2: Sl st in first 2-ch space, work one petal [1 dc, 3 tr, 1 dc] in each 2-ch space to end of rnd, join with a sl st in base of 1 dc at beg of rnd. *(6 petals)*
Cont working next rnd at back of work.
Round 3: 3 ch, miss first petal, *ss in back of first dc of next petal, 3 ch; rep from * to end of rnd, join with a sl st in first ch of rnd. *(6 3-ch space)*
Round 4: Sl st in first 3-ch space, work one petal [1 dc, 5 tr, 1 dc] in each 3-ch space to end of rnd, join with a sl st in base of 1 dc at beg of rnd. *(6 petals)*
Change to Col A.
Numbering petals from start of rnd, work Round 5 as folls:
Round 5: 3 ch, miss first petal, sl st in back of centre st of second petal, 3 ch, miss third petal, sl st in back of first dc of fourth petal, 3 ch, sl st in back of centre st of fifth petal, 3 ch, join with a sl st in first ch of rnd. *(4 ch3-sp)*
Round 6: 3 ch (counts as 1 tr), in 3-ch sp at base of 3-ch work [2 tr, 3 ch, 3 tr] 1 ch, *work in next 3-ch space [3 tr, 3 ch, 3 tr], 1 ch; rep from * to end of rnd, join with a sl st in top of 3-ch at beg of rnd.

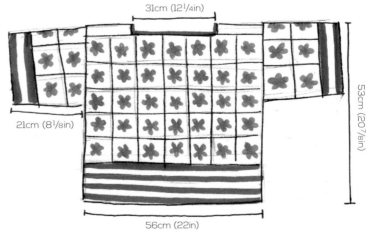

31cm (12¼in)

21cm (8⅛in)

53cm (20⅞in)

56cm (22in)

Round 7: Sl st to next 3-ch space, 3 ch (counts as 1 tr), in 3-ch space at base of 3-ch work [2 tr, 3 ch, 3 tr] 1 ch, *work in next 1ch-sp 3 tr, 1 ch, work in next 3ch-sp [3 tr, 3 ch, 3 tr], 1 ch; rep from * twice more, 1 ch, work in next 1-ch space 3 tr, 1 ch, join with a sl st in top of 3-ch at beg of rnd.

Round 8: Sl st to next 3-ch space, 3 ch (counts as 1 tr), in 3-ch space at base of 3-ch work [2 tr, 3 ch, 3 tr] 1 ch, cont working in patt as set; work in each corner space [3 tr, 3 ch, 3 tr, 1 ch]; work in each 1-ch space [3 tr, 1 ch], join with a sl st in top of 3-ch at beg of rnd.
Break yarn and fasten off.

BLOCK THE MEADOW SQUARES

Spray block each individual meadow square to even out the stitches and achieve a perfectly square shape. Place each meadow square onto a blocking mat or flat surface covered with a towel, then spritz each square with a generous amount of water from a spray bottle. Pin the corners of each meadow square to the blocking mat, making sure each side measures 8cm (3⅛in) and opposite sides are parallel. Add more pins along each edge of the meadow squares to keep them straight. Once the meadow squares completely dry, remove the pins.

JOIN THE MEADOW SQUARES

Once you have finished and blocked all 90 squares, stitch together five rows of seven squares and then stitch these five rows together along the long edges to create a block of 35 squares for the Front. Repeat with another 35 squares for the Back. For the Sleeves, stitch together two rows of five squares and then stitch these squares together along the long edge to create a block of 10 squares. Repeat for the second Sleeve.

ADD STRIPED EDGING

Cont working in rows, turning at end of each row, along bottom edge of Front panel, work as folls:
Row 1: With RS facing, along bottom edge of row of seven squares, with a 4mm (US size G/6) crochet hook and using Col C, 2 ch, 1 dc in 3-ch space, 1 dc in each st and seam along edge, 1 dc in last 3-ch space. *(113 sts)*
Row 2: 3 ch, (counts as first tr), 1 tr in each st to end of row.
Row 3: Work as Row 2.
Rows 4–5: Change to Col A, rep Rows 2–3.
Rows 6–7: Change to Col C, rep Rows 2–3.
Rep rows 4–5 twice more, finishing with a Col C stripe.
Break yarn and fasten off.
Repeat on Back panel.

Cont working in rows, turning at end of each row, along bottom edge of Sleeve panel, work as folls:
Row 1: With RS facing, along bottom edge of row of five squares, using 4mm (US size G/6) crochet hook and Col C, 2 ch, 1 dc in 3-ch space, 1 dc in each st and seam along edge, 1 dc in last 3-ch space. *(81 sts)*
Row 2: 3 ch, (counts as first tr), 1 tr in each st to end of row.
Row 3: Work as Row 2.
Rows 4–5: Change to Col A, rep Rows 2–3.
Rows 6–7: Change to Col C, rep Rows 2–3.
Break yarn and fasten off.
Repeat on other Sleeve panel.

SHAPE NECK ON FRONT AND BACK PANELS

Cont working in rows, turning at end of each row, as folls:
Row 1: With WS facing, using 4mm (US size G/6) crochet hook and Col A, as for bottom edge 2 ch, 1 dc in each st across top edge of panel. *(113 sts)*
Next row: 3 ch (counts as first tr), 1 tr in each of next 27 sts, turn. *(28 sts)*
Next row: 3 ch (counts as first tr), 1 tr in each st to end of row.
Break yarn and fasten off.
With RS facing, count 28 sts from lefthand edge, rejoin yarn to other side of neck with a 3 ch (counts as first tr), 1 tr in each of next 27 sts from shoulder edge. *(28 sts)*
Next row: 3 ch (counts as first tr), 1 tr in each of next 27 sts to neck edge.
Break yarn and fasten off.

TO FINISH

Weave any loose yarn ends into the back of your work so they are not visible from the right side.
Lightly steam all the garment pieces.
Seam together the Back and Fronts at the shoulders.
Fold the Sleeves in half lengthways to mark the centre point, then pin the centre of the sleeveheads to the shoulder seams and stitch in place.
Sew the Back and Fronts together along the side seams, stitching from the bottom edge of the garment up to the underarm, then down along the underarm Sleeve seams to the cuffs.

ADD NECK EDGING

Using a 4mm (US size G/6) crochet hook and Col C, rejoin yarn to any point along back of neckline, 2 ch.
Work 1 dc in each st around neckline, join rnd with a sl st in top of 2-ch.
Break yarn and fasten off.
Weave in any loose yarn ends.

VINTAGE-STYLE EMBROIDERED TOP

///

YOU WILL NEED

YARN
8(8:8:9:9) x 50g (1¾oz) balls of Drops *Alpaca 4ply*,
or a similar 4ply-weight wool yarn, in pale blue
(6205 Light Blue)

OTHER MATERIALS
Embroidery threads in selection of colours

CROCHET HOOK
3.25mm (US size D/3) crochet hook

OTHER EQUIPMENT
Blunt-ended needle or tapestry needle for weaving in yarn
ends and seaming
Embroidery needles

TENSION
3.5 fan stitch repeats and 4 rows to 10cm (4in) measured
over fan stitch pattern using 3.25mm (US size D/3)
crochet hook

ABBREVIATIONS
See page 9

SIZE (UK)	6	8	10	12	14	16
To fit bust (cm)	76	81	86	91	97	102
To fit bust (in)	30	32	34	36	38	40
Actual bust (cm)	92	97	102	107	113	118
Actual bust (in)	36¼	38¼	40	42	44½	46½
Length (cm)	48	48	48	50	50	52
Length (in)	19	19	19	19¾	19¾	20½

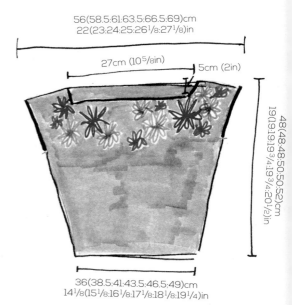

56(58.5:61:63.5:66.5:69)cm
22(23:24:25:26¹/₈:27¹/₈)in

27cm (10⅝in)   5cm (2in)

48(48:48:50:50:52)cm
19(19:19:19¾:19¾:20½)in

36(38.5:41:43.5:46.5:49)cm
14¹/₈(15¹/₈:16¹/₈:17¹/₈:18¹/₈:19¼)in

FRONT

Foundation row: Using a 3.25mm (US size D/3) crochet hook, make 104(112:120:128:136:144) chain + 1 chain.

Cont working in rows, turning at end of each row.

Row 1 (RS): 1 dc in second ch from hook, *miss 3 ch, work 9-tr shell in next ch, miss 3 ch, 1 dc in next ch; rep from * to end, turn.

Row 2: 3 ch (counts as first tr), 1 tr in next st, *5 ch, miss 9-tr shell, work a V-st of [1 tr, 1 ch, 1 tr] in next dc; rep from * ending 5 ch, miss last 9-tr shell, 2 tr in last dc, miss tch, turn.

Row 3: 3 ch (counts as first tr), 4 tr in first st, *working over next 5-ch to enclose it, work 1 dc in fifth tr of 9-tr shell in row below **, 9-tr shell in space at centre of next V-st; rep from * ending last rep at **, 5 tr in top of tch, turn.

Row 4: 3 ch, miss 5 tr, V-st in next dc, *5 ch, miss 9-tr shell, V-st in next dc; rep from * ending 2 ch, sl st to top of tch, turn.

Row 5: 1 ch, miss sl st and 2 ch, 1 dc in next st, *work 9-tr shell in space at centre of next V-st **, working over next 5-ch to enclose it, work 1 dc in fifth dc of 9-tr shell in row below; rep from * ending last rep at **, 1 dc in first ch of tch, turn.

Rep rows 2–5 a further 3(3:3:4:4:5) times.

Work a set of inc rows as folls:

Row 1: Work as Row 2 of st patt.

Row 2: Work as Row 3, but working 3rd (3rd:4th:4th:5th:5th) 9-tr shell by working [5 tr, 1 ch, 5 tr] in sp where 9 tr would go, cont in st patt until 3rd (3rd:4th:4th:5th:5th) full 9-tr shells from end and work in the same way [5 tr, 1 ch, 5 tr], work to end of row.

Row 3: Work as Row 4 but when you reach split shells work [5 ch, V-st in ch sp in bet two 5 tr, 5 ch].

Row 4: Work as Row 5 of st patt.

Work rows 2–5 without shaping a further 4 times.
Work inc Rows 1–4 and Rows 2–5 of stitch pattern without shaping a further 4 times. ***
Work inc Rows 1–4 once more.
Work Rows 2–5 of stitch pattern without shaping a further 3 times.

Next row (WS): Work in place of 5ch bet V-sts [2 ch, sl st to fifth tr of 9-tr shell, 2 ch].

SHAPE NECK
Work each side separately.

Row 1: Work as Row 3 of st patt: work [9-tr shells] 5 times then 2 tr in ch of next V-st, turn.

Row 2: Work as Row 4: 3 ch, sl st in fifth tr of 9-tr shell, 2 ch, V-st, work to end of row.

Row 3: Work as Row 5: work [9-tr shells] 5 times, 1 dc in sl st of previous row.

Next work Rows 2–5 of st patt one more time and then work final row as folls:

Next row (WS): Work in place of 5ch bet V-sts [2 ch, sl st to fifth tr of 9-tr shell, 2 ch].

Break yarn and fasten off.

Row 1: With RS facing, rejoin yarn to other side of neck, work five full 9-tr shells from end of row, 3 ch, 1 tr in ch of V-st, work as Row 3 of patt, work [9-tr shells] 5 times, then 5 tr in top of tch, turn.

Row 2: Work as Row 4 of st patt, work to last V-st, 2 ch, sl st in fifth tr of 9-tr shell, 1 tr in top of tch, turn.

Row 3: Work as Row 5 of st patt, work [9-tr shells] 5 times, 1 dc in sl st from previous row.

Next work Rows 2–5 of st patt one more time and then work final row as folls:

Next row (WS): Work in place of 5-ch bet V-sts [2 ch, sl st to fifth tr of 9-tr shell, 2 ch].

Break yarn and fasten off.

BACK

Foundation row: Using a 3.25mm (US size D/3) crochet hook, make 104(112:120:128:136:144) chain + 1 chain.

Work as Front patt until ***.

Work inc Rows 1–4 once more.

Work rows 2–5 of stitch pattern without shaping a further 5 times.

Next row (WS): Work in place of 5-ch bet V-sts [2 ch, sl st to fifth tr of 9-tr shell, 2 ch].

Break yarn and fasten off.

TO FINISH

Weave any loose yarn ends into the back of your work so they are not visible from the right side.

Lightly steam all the garment pieces.

Seam together the Back and Fronts at the shoulders.

Next, sew the side seams, leaving openings for the armholes. The armhole openings can be as wide as you like; I prefer to leave the top third unstitched for the armhole openings so the top drapes nicely.

Work a round of double crochet around the neckline and the armhole openings in either the main colour or a contrast colour yarn.

Add some embroidery stitches to the Front of the top in whichever designs and colours you prefer. I embroidered clusters of chain stitches in varying sizes and shades to form the floral motifs, which is really quick and easy way of adding splashes of colour to your crochet.

FLORAL SUMMER TOP

YOU WILL NEED

YARN
2 x 245g (8⅝oz) cones of Yeoman Yarns *Cannele 4ply*, or a similar 4ply-weight cotton yarn, in white (6 White)

CROCHET HOOK
2.5mm (US size 1/0) crochet hook

OTHER EQUIPMENT
Blunt-ended needle or tapestry needle for weaving in yarn ends and seaming

TENSION
One Large Floral Motif once finished and blocked measures 6cm (2⅜in) in diameter

ABBREVIATIONS
See page 9

SPECIAL ABBREVIATION
qtr (quadruple treble) = wrap yarn four times around hook before making stitch, insert hook in chain space and pull up a loop, wrap yarn around hook and draw yarn through two loops at a time (as for all treble stitches) until one loop left on hook.

DESIGN NOTE
This top is simple to make but takes a fair bit of sewing together once you have completed all your Large and Small Floral Motifs.

SIZE (UK)	SMALL 6–8	MEDIUM 10–12	LARGE 14–18
To fit bust (cm)	81	91	102
To fit bust (in)	32	36	40
Actual bust (cm)	92	101	110
Actual bust (in)	36	40	43½
Length (cm)	61	61	61
Length (in)	24	24	24

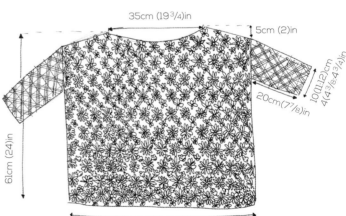

35cm (19¾)in

5cm (2)in

10(11:12)cm 4(4⅜:4¾)in

20cm(7⅞)in

61cm (24)in

110(120:130)cm all the way round
43¼(47¼:51⅛)in all the way round

55(60:65)cm when laid flat
21⅝(23⅝:25⅝)cm when laid flat

LARGE FLORAL MOTIFS (MAKE 166(184:202))

Begin with a magic circle as foundation ring.

Cont working in rounds, with RS always facing.

Round 1: 8 dc in centre of ring, pull tight and join with a sl st in top of first dc.

Round 2: 2 ch, *1 htr in next dc, 2 ch; rep from * a further 6 times, join with a sl st in top of 2ch.

Round 3: 1 ch, *work [1 dc, 6 ch, 1 qtr, 6 ch, 1 dc] in next ch space; rep from * in each ch space to end of rnd, join with a sl st in top of first dc.

Break yarn and fasten off.

SMALL FLORAL MOTIFS (MAKE 152(170:188))

Begin with a magic circle as foundation ring.

Cont working in rounds, with RS always facing.

Round 1: [1 dc, 2 ch, 1 tr, 2 ch, 1 dc] 5 times in centre of ring, pull tight.

Break yarn and fasten off.

SLEEVES (MAKE 2)

Using a 2.5mm (US size 1/0) crochet hook, make 52(56:60) chain + 2 chain.

Cont working in rows, turning at end of each row.

Row 1: 1 dc in second ch from hook, *2 ch, in same ch as 1 dc work 1 tr until two loops rem on hook, miss 3 ch, work 1 tr in next ch until three loops rem on hook, yo and through all three loops, 2 ch, 1 dc in same ch as last tr (one cluster made); rep from * to end of row, turn. *(13(14:15) cls)*

Row 2: 3 ch (counts as first tr), work 1 tr in top of first cl, *2 ch, in same cl as last tr work [1 dc, 2 ch, 1 tr until two loops rem on hook], 1 tr in top of next cl until three loops rem on hook, yo and through all three loops; rep from * to end placing last tr in last dc, turn.

Row 3: 1 ch, in first cl work [1 dc, 2 ch, 1 tr until two loops rem on hook], 1 tr in top of next cl until three loops rem on hook, yo and through all three loops, *2 ch, in same cl as last tr work [1 dc, 2 ch, 1 tr until two loops rem on hook], 1 tr in next cl until three loops rem on hook, yo and through all three loops; rep from * to end, 2 ch, 1 dc in third ch of 3-ch at beg of previous row, turn.

Rows 2 and 3 form st patt for Sleeve.

Rows 4–5: Rep Rows 2–3 one more time.

Work incs as folls:

Row 6: 4 ch (counts as 1 tr + 1 ch), cont in stitch pattern as set to end of row, turn.

Row 7: 2 ch, cont in stitch pattern as set to end of row, working last dc in third ch of 4-ch at beg of previous row, turn.

Row 8: 4 ch (counts as 1 tr + 1 ch), work in st patt as set to end of row, placing last tr in second ch of 2-ch at beg of previous row, turn.

Row 9: Rep Row 7.

The number of cls rems the same throughout but as the Sleeve widens more edge stitches become longer – replace the first tr with a dtr and first 2 ch with a 3 ch of each row as folls:

Row 10: 3 ch (counts as 1 tr + 1 ch), work 1 dtr in top of first cl, 3 ch, cont in st patt as set on previous rows to end of row, placing last tr in second ch of 2-ch at beg of previous row, turn.

Row 11: 2 ch, in first cl work [1 dc, 3 ch, 1 dtr until two lps rem on hook], cont in st patt as set on previous rows to end of row, working last dc in third ch of 4-ch at beg of previous row, turn.

Rows 12–16: Rep Rows 10–11 twice more and Row 10 once more.

Row 17: Maintaining incs made so far, make second tr in a 1 dtr and second 2-ch in a 3 ch, work to end of row, rep these incs at end of row.

Rows 18–20: Maintaining all incs, work stitch pattern without shaping to end of row.

Row 21 (inc row): Replace third tr with 1 dtr and third 2-ch with 3 ch, work to end of row, rep incs at end of row.

Row 22: Maintaining all incs, work stitch pattern without shaping to end of row.

Row 23 (inc row): Replace fourth tr with 1 dtr and fourth 2-ch with 3 ch, work to end of row, rep incs at end of row.

Rows 24–26: Maintaining all incs, work stitch pattern without shaping to end of row.

Break yarn and fasten off.

TO FINISH

Arrange the large floral motifs each like a compass, with the petals pointing north, east, south and west. Sew the cardinal points of each neighbouring motif together so that south meets north, east meets west, and so on. Stitch these larger motifs over the shoulders so the Front and Back are joined, leaving a neck opening approx 35cm (13¾in) wide and create a nice scooped neckline. Sew a small floral motif into the space between four large motifs. Match each of the unattached petals of the surrounding four large motifs to a petal of the small motif leaving the fifth petal of the small motif pointing north on the fabric. Make sure the large motifs are always sitting at the edge of the fabric and just fill out the inner spaces of the large motifs. Once all your motifs are joined together, stitch the top of the sleeve across the shoulders from the front to the back, so each sleeve sits equally on the front and back. Sew the Back and Fronts together along the side seams, joining these motifs together, stitching from the bottom edge of the garment up to the underarm, then down along the underarm Sleeve seams.

⁺STRIPED SHIFT DRESS

YOU WILL NEED

YARN
4(5:5) x 50g (1¾oz) balls BC Garn *Semilla Organic DK*, or a similar double-knitting-weight wool yarn, in each of three colours:
A dark blue (114 Dark Blue)
B mustard (107 Relish)
C orange (115 Burnt Orange)

CROCHET HOOKS
4mm and 4.5mm (US size G/6 and 7) crochet hooks

OTHER EQUIPMENT
Blunt-ended needle or tapestry needle for weaving in yarn ends and seaming

TENSION
3 stars and 7–8 rows to 10cm (4in) measured over stitch pattern using a 4mm (US size G/6) crochet hook
One full star stitch measures 4.5cm (1¾in) wide
One half star stitch measures 2.5cm (1in) wide

ABBREVIATIONS
See page 9

SPECIAL ABBREVIATION
tr2tog = work 2 trebles in next stitch until one loop of each remains on hook, yarn over and draw through all three loops on hook

STRIPE PATTERN
Rows 1–2: Col A.
Rows 3–5: Col B.
Rows 6–8: Col C.
Cont changing colour yarn as set after every third row.

STITCH PATTERN
Cont working in rows, turning at end of each row.
Row 1 (RS): 1 dc in second ch from hook, 1 ch, miss 1 ch, 1 dc in next ch, [3 ch, miss 3 ch, 1 dc in next ch] twice, *2 ch, miss 2 ch, 1 dc in next ch, [3 ch, miss 3 ch, 1 dc in next ch] twice; rep from * to last 2 ch, 1 ch, miss 1 ch, 1 dc in last ch, turn.
Row 2: 3 ch, in first ch space work [tr2tog, 2 ch, tr2tog], 1 ch, miss 1 dc, 1 dc in next dc, *1 ch, miss 3-ch space, tr2tog in next 2-ch space, in same space as last tr2tog work [2 ch, tr2tog] three times, 1 ch, miss 3-ch space, 1 dc in next dc; rep from * to last 2 spaces, 1 ch, miss 3-ch space, in last ch space work [tr2tog, 2 ch, tr2tog], 1 tr in last dc, turn.

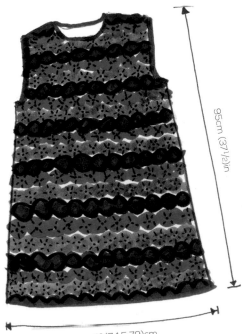

95cm (37½)in

70(74.5:79)cm
27½(29⅜:31⅜)in

SIZE (UK)	SMALL 6–8	MEDIUM 10–12	LARGE 16–18
To fit bust (cm)	81	91	102
To fit bust (in)	32	36	40
Actual bust (cm)	92	101	110
Actual bust (in)	36	40	43½
Length (cm)	95	95	95
Length (in)	37½	37½	37½

Row 3: 1 ch, 1 dc in first tr, *3 ch, work tr2tog in top of each of next 4tr2tog, 3 ch, 1 dc in next 2-ch space; rep from * to end placing last dc in third of 3-ch at beg of previous row, turn.
Row 4: 1 ch, 1 dc in first dc, *3 ch, 1 dc in top of next tr2tog, 2 ch, miss 2tr2tog, 1 dc in top of next tr2tog, 3 ch, 1 dc in next dc; rep from * to end, turn.
Row 5: 1 ch, work 1 dc in first dc, *1 ch, miss 3-ch space, tr2tog in next 2-ch space, in same space as last tr2tog work [2ch, tr2tog] 3 times, 1 ch, miss 3-ch space, 1 dc in next dc; rep from * to end, turn.
Row 6: 3 ch, work tr2tog in top of each of next 2tr2tog, 3 ch, 1 dc in next 2-ch space, 3 ch, *tr2tog in top of each 4tr2tog, 3 ch, 1 dc in next 2-ch space, 3 ch; rep from * to last 2tr2tog, work tr2tog in each of last 2tr2tog, 1 tr in last dc, turn.
Row 7: 1 ch, 1 dc in first tr, 1 ch, miss tr2tog, 1 dc in next tr2tog, 3 ch, 1 dc in next dc, 3 ch, *1 dc in top of next tr2tog, 2 ch, miss 2tr2tog, 1 dc in top of next tr2tog, 3 ch, 1 dc in next dc, 3 ch; rep from * to last 2tr2tog, 1 dc in next tr2tog, 1 ch, miss tr2tog, 1 dc in third of 3-ch at beg of previous row, turn.
Rows 2–7 form st patt. Rep these rows throughout.

FRONT

Foundation row: Using a 4.5mm (US size 7) crochet hook and Col A, make 165(176:187) chain + 3 chain. Change to a 4mm (US size G/6) crochet hook.
Row 1: 1 dc in fourth ch from hook, 1 ch, miss 1 ch, 1 dc in next ch, [3 ch, miss 3 ch, 1 dc in next ch] twice, *2 ch, miss 2 ch, 1 dc in next ch, [3 ch, miss 3 ch, 1 dc in next ch] twice; rep from * to last 2 ch, 1 ch, miss 1 ch, 1 dc in last ch, turn.
Row 2: 3 ch (does NOT count as stitch), 2trtog in same st as 3-ch and next ch space, 1 htr in dc, 1 htr in 3-ch space, 2 dc in 3-ch space, in next tr work st patt Row 5 from first dc, work in patt to last 3-ch space, [2 sc, 1 htr] in 3-ch space, 1 htr in dc, 2trtog in next ch space and last st, turn.
Row 3: 1 ch, 1 tr, 2 htr, dc2tog, work st patt Row 6 to last 5 sts, dc2tog, 2 htr, 1 tr, turn.
Row 4: 1 ch, 1 dc in each of next 4 sts, work st patt Row 7 to last 4 sts, 1 dc in each of next 4 sts, turn.
Row 5: 1 ch, 1 tr, htr2tog, 1 dc, work st patt Row 2 to last 4 sts, 1 dc, 2htr2tog, 1 tr, turn.
Row 6: 3 ch, 1 tr and 1htr2tog, 1 dc, work st patt Row 3 to last 3 sts, 1 dc, 1 htr and 1trtog, turn.
Row 7: 1 ch, 2 dc, work st patt Row 4 to last 2 sts, 2 dc, turn.
Row 8: 3 ch, 1 tr and 1htrtog, work st patt Row 5 to last 2 sts, 1 htr and 1trtog, turn.
Row 9: [2 tr, 2 htr, 1 dc, dc2tog] over top of first half star, work st patt Row 6 to last half star st, [dc2tog, 1 dc, 2 htr, 2 tr] over last half star st, turn.
Row 10: 1 ch, 6 dc, work st patt Row 7 to last 6 sts, 6 dc, turn.
Rep Rows 2–10 until a total of 63 rows (65 including the foundation and row 1) have been worked, ending with Col B. (You now have 20 star rows and 2 half star rows at beg and end.)
Starting with st patt Row 5, cont working 15 rows in st patt with no variation from instructions.
Break yarn and fasten off.
SHAPE NECK AND ARMHOLE
Work each side separately.
Rejoin Col B yarn at side edge.
Row 1: Miss one star (join in centre of star), work st patt Row 2 to centre of last full star, turn.
Row 2: Work st patt Row 3, turn.
Row 3: Work st patt Row 4, turn.
Row 4: 4 ch, miss 3-ch space and 1 tr, work st patt Row 2 (replacing 3 ch with 1 tr) in 2-ch space, leave last 1 tr and 3-ch space unworked, turn.
***
Leaving 3(4:5) stars unworked in centre front, work each side of neck separately, starting at armhole edge.
Cont working in st patt, starting with a st patt Row 3, for a further 12 rows and at the same time dec by one 2trtog on the 1st and every foll 3rd row (st patt rows: 3, 6, 3, 6).
SHAPE SHOULDER
Cont working in st patt for a further 2 rows.
Work a final row but exchanging all sts for dc over first star and for htr over second star to create a slope.
Break yarn and fasten off.
Rejoin Col B yarn to other side edge and rep neck and armhole shaping, reversing all shaping.

BACK

Work as given for Front to ***.
Work a further 9 rows in st patt straight with no dec.
SHAPE NECK
Work each side of neck separately.
Starting at side edge, work a further 3 rows in st patt, leaving centre three stars unworked.
Work shoulder shaping as given for Front.

TO FINISH

Weave in any loose yarn ends to the back of your work so that they are not visible from the right side.
Seam together the Front and Back at the shoulders.
Sew the Front and Back together along the side seams, carefully matching the stripes.

FAN STITCH CARDIGAN

//

YOU WILL NEED

YARN
9(11) x 50g (1¾oz) balls of BC Garn *Semilla Organic Grosso*, or a similar aran-weight wool yarn, in bright pink (123 Pop Pink)

OTHER MATERIALS
Five 2cm (⅞in) diameter buttons

CROCHET HOOKS
6mm (US size J/10) crochet hook

OTHER EQUIPMENT
Blunt-ended needle or tapestry needle for weaving in yarn ends and seaming

TENSION
One full pattern repeat measures approximately 6.5cm (2¼in) wide and 6.25cm (2⅜in) tall

ABBREVIATIONS
See page 9

SIZE (UK)	S–M	L–XL
To fit bust (cm)	Up to 91	Up to 116
To fit bust (in)	Up to 36	Up to 46
Actual bust (cm)	84	110
Actual bust (in)	33	43½
Length (cm)	50	50
Length (in)	19¾	19¾
Sleeve seam (cm)	22	22
Sleeve seam (in)	8½	8½

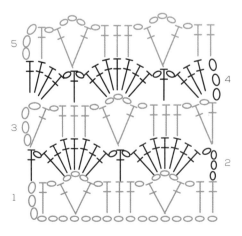

Fan Stitch chart

BACK

Foundation row: Using a 6mm (US size J/10) crochet hook, make 56(64) chain + 3 chain.

Cont working in rows, turning at end of each row.

Row 1 (WS): 1 tr in fourth ch from hook, *1ch, miss 2 ch, in next ch work [1 tr, 3 ch, 1 tr], 1 ch, miss 2 ch, 1 tr in each of next 3 ch; rep from * to end missing 1 tr at end of last rep, turn.

Row 2: 4 ch (counts as first tr and 1 ch), work 7 tr in next 3-ch space, *1 ch, miss 2 tr, 1 tr in next 1 tr, 1 ch, 7 tr in next 3-ch space; rep from * to last 3 tr, 1 ch, miss 2 tr, 1 tr in top of 3 ch, turn.

Row 3: 4 ch (counts as first tr and 1 ch), 1 tr in next tr, 1 ch, miss 2 tr, 1 tr in each of next 3 tr, *1 ch, miss 2 tr, in next tr work [1 tr, 3 ch, 1 tr], 1 ch, miss 2 tr, 1 tr in each of next 3 tr; rep from * to last 3 tr, miss 2 tr, in third of 4 ch at beg of previous row work [1 tr, 1 ch, 1 tr], turn.

Row 4: 3 ch (counts as first tr), 3 tr in first ch space, 1 ch, miss 2 tr, 1 tr in next tr, *1 ch, 7 tr in next 3-ch space, 1 ch, miss 2 tr, 1 tr in next tr; rep from * to last 3 tr, 1 ch, miss 2 tr, 3 tr in last ch space, 1 tr in third of 4 ch at beg of previous row, turn.

Row 5: 3 ch (counts as first tr), miss 1 tr, 1 tr in next tr, *1 ch, miss 2 tr, in next tr work [1 tr, 3 ch, 1 tr], 1 ch, miss 2 tr, 1 tr in each of next 3 tr; rep from * to end missing 1 tr at end of last rep and working last tr in third of 3ch at beg of previous row, turn.

Rep Rows 2–5 a further 4 times.

SHAPE ARMHOLE

Row 1: Work as Row 2 of stitch pattern: sl st in each of next 2 tr, 3 ch (counts as first tr), 1 tr in second arm of V-st, work in patt to last V-st of row, 1 tr in first arm of V-st, 1 tr in second arm of V-st, turn.

Row 2: Work as Row 3 of st patt: 3 ch (counts as first tr), V-st in 1 tr bet ch, work in st patt to end of row, ending after last V-st, 1 tr in top of 3ch of previous row, turn.

Row 3: Work as Row 4 of st patt: 3 ch (counts as first tr), 3 tr in 3-ch space, work in st patt to last 3-ch space, 3 tr in 3-ch space, 1 tr in top of 3ch of previous row, turn.

Row 4: Work as Row 5 of st patt: 3 ch, 1 tr in second st, work in st patt to last 2 sts (including tch), 1 tr in each st.

Rep Rows 2–5 of st patt a further 2 times then rep Rows 2–3 one more time.

Break yarn and fasten off.

LEFT FRONT

Foundation row: Using a 6mm (US size J/10) crochet hook, make 32(40) chain + 3 chain.

Work Rows 1–5 as given for Back.

Work Rows 2–5 only as given for Back a further 4 times.

SHAPE ARMHOLE

Row 1: Work as Row 2 of stitch pattern: sl st in each of next 2 tr, 3 ch, 1 tr in second arm of V-st, work in stitch pattern to end of row, turn.

Row 2: Work as Row 3 of stitch pattern: work in stitch pattern to end of row, ending after last V-st, 1 tr in top of 3ch of previous row.

Row 3: Work as Row 4 of stitch pattern: 3 ch, 3 tr in

14cm(5½)in
16cm(6¼)in
50cm(19¾)in
21cm(8¼)in
84(110)cm
33⅛(43¼)in

3ch-sp, work in stitch pattern to end of row.
Row 4: Work as Row 5 of st patt: 3 ch, 1 tr in second st, work in st patt to last 2 sts (including tch), 1 tr in each st.
SHAPE NECK
Row 1: Work as Row 2 of st patt: work in stitch pattern to last V-st, 1 tr in first arm of V-st, turn.
Row 2: Work as Row 3: 3 ch, miss 1 st, 2 tr in next tr, work in stitch pattern to end of row, turn.
Row 3: Work as Row 4: work in stitch pattern to last 3 sts, 1 tr in next st, miss 1 st, 1 tr in top of tch, turn.
Row 4: Work as Row 5: 3 ch, miss 1 ch, work V-st in 1 tr of previous row, work in stitch pattern to end of row, turn.
Row 5: Work as Row 2: work in stitch pattern to last 3ch-sp, 3 tr in 3ch-sp, 1 tr in top of tch, turn.
Row 6: Work as Row 3: 3 ch, 1 tr in centre st of 3 tr from previous row, work in stitch pattern to end of row, turn.
Row 7: Work as Row 4: work in stitch pattern to final 3ch-sp, 7 tr in 3ch-sp, 1 ch, 1 tr in top of tch.
Row 8: 4ch, 1 tr in first tr, work in st patt to end of row.
Rows 9–10: Work in stitch pattern as set.
Break yarn and fasten off.

RIGHT FRONT

Foundation row: Using a 6mm (US size J/10) crochet hook, make 32(40) chain + 3 chain.
Work Rows 1–5 as given for Back.
Work Rows 2–5 only as given for Back a further 4 times.
SHAPE ARMHOLE
Row 1: Work as Row 2 of st patt: work in stitch pattern to last V-st of row, 1 tr in first arm of V-st, 1 tr in second

arm, turn.
Row 2: Work as Row 3: 3 ch, go straight in V-st in 1 tr bet chs, work in stitch pattern to end of row.
Row 3: Work as Row 4: work in stitch pattern to last 3-ch space, 3 tr in 3-ch space, 1 tr in top of 3ch of previous row.
Row 4: Work as Row 5: 3 ch, 1 tr in second st, work in stitch pattern to last 2 sts (including tch), 1 tr in each st.
SHAPE NECK
Row 1: Work as Row 2: sl st to second arm of first V-st, 4 ch, 1 tr in centre st of 3 tr, work in st patt to end of row.
Row 2: Work as Row 3: work to last 1 tr, 2 tr in 1 tr of previous row, 1 tr in top of tch, turn.
Row 3: Work as Row 4 : 4 ch, 1 tr in second tr, 1 ch, 1 tr in centre st of 3 tr, work in stitch pattern to end of row.
Row 4: Work as Row 5: work to last V-st of row, work V-st, work 1 tr in top of tch, turn.
Row 5: Work as Row 2: 3 ch, 3 tr in 3ch-sp of V-st, work in stitch pattern to end of row, turn.
Row 6: Work as Row 3: work to last V-st of row, 1 ch, 1 tr in centre st of 3 tr of previous row, 1 tr in top of tch, turn.
Row 7: Work as Row 4: 4 ch, 7 tr in 3ch-sp, work in stitch pattern to end of row.
Rows 8–10: Work in stitch pattern as set.
Break yarn and fasten off.

SLEEVES (MAKE 2)

Foundation row: Using a 6mm (US size J/10) crochet hook, make 40(48) chain + 3 chain.

Work Rows 1–5 as given for Back.
Work Rows 2–5 only as given for Back a further 3 times.

SHAPE SLEEVEHEAD

Row 1: Work as Row 2 of stitch pattern: sl st across to second arm of first V-st, 4 ch, 1 tr in centre st of 3 tr of previous row, work in patt to last V-st of previous row, 1 tr in first arm, turn.

Row 2: Work as Row 3 of stitch pattern: 3 ch, work V-st in next 1 tr, work in patt to last V-st, 1 tr in top of tch, turn.

Row 3: Work as Row 4 of stitch pattern: 3 ch, 3 tr in 3ch-sp, work in patt to last 3ch-sp, 3 tr in sp, 1 tr in top of tch, turn.

Row 4: Work as Row 5 of stitch pattern: 4 ch, work V-st in next 1 tr, work in patt to last V-st, 1 ch, 1 tr in top of tch, turn.

Row 5: Work as Row 2 of stitch pattern: 3ch, 3 tr in 3ch-sp, work in patt to last 3ch-sp, 3 tr in next sp, 1 tr in top of tch, turn.

Row 6: Work as Row 3 of stitch pattern: 4 ch, work V-st in next 1 tr, work in patt to last V-st, 1 ch, 1 tr in top of tch, turn.

Row 7: Work as Row 4 of stitch pattern: 3 ch, 2 tr in 3ch-sp, work in patt to last 3ch-sp, 2 tr in next sp, 1 tr in top of tch.

Row 8: Work as Row 5 of stitch pattern: 3 ch, miss 1 st, 1 tr in next st, work in patt to last 3 sts, 1 tr, miss 1 st, 1 tr in top of tch.
Break yarn and fasten off.

PATCH POCKETS (MAKE 2)

Foundation row: Using a 6mm (US size J/10) crochet hook, make 16 chain + 3 chain.
Work Rows 1–5 as given for Back.
Work Rows 2–3 only as given for Back.
Break yarn and fasten off.

TO FINISH

Weave in any loose ends into the back of your work so they are not visible from the RS.

Begin by sewing together the shoulder seams then pin the sleeveheads into the armhole spaces before sewing them into place.

Finally, stitch up the side seams by sewing the front and back pieces together up to the underarm stitch up along the sleeve. Stitch on your patch pockets.

ADD NECK TRIM

With RS facing and begin at centre front of Right Front, insert hook and 3 ch, work tr all the way round to centre front of Left Front.
Break yarn and fasten off.

ADD BUTTON BAND TO LEFT FRONT

With RS facing, rejoin yarn to top front edge of Left Front, make 3 chain, work tr evenly all the way down front edge and then across bottom edge, turn.
Cont working in rows, turning at end of each row.
Next row (WS): 1 ch, 1 dc in each st to end of row.
Next row: 3 ch, 1 tr in each st to end of row.
Break yarn and fasten off.

ADD BUTTONHOLE BAND TO RIGHT FRONT

On Right Front place markers at your preferred position for the buttonholes so you can work in the correct places.
With RS facing, rejoin yarn to bottom front edge of Right Front, make 3 chain, work tr evenly all the way up front edge, turn.
Cont working in rows, turning at end of each row.
Next row: 1 ch, *1 dc in each st to next button marker, 1 ch, miss 1 st; rep from * to last marker, 1 dc in each st to end of row.
Next row: 3 ch, 1 tr in each st to end of row.
Break yarn and fasten off.
Sew buttons on Left Front button band to match buttonholes on Right Front.

DAISY SWING COAT

YOU WILL NEED

YARN
Wool And The Gang *Shiny Happy Cotton*, or a similar bulky-weight cotton yarn, in three colours:
A 12(12:12:12:13:13:13) x 100g (3½oz) balls in bright blue (True Blue)
B 1(1:1:1:1:1) x 100g (3½oz) ball in bright yellow (Yellow Brick Road)
C 1(1:1:1:1:1) x 100g (3½oz) ball in white (White Noise)

CROCHET HOOK
5mm (US size H/8) crochet hook

OTHER EQUIPMENT
Blunt-ended needle or tapestry needle for weaving in yarn ends and seaming

TENSION
18 sts and 22 rows to 10cm measured over double crochet using a 5mm (US Size H/8) crochet hook

ABBREVIATIONS
See page 9

SIZE (UK)	6	8	10	12	14	16
To fit bust (cm)	76	81	86	91	97	102
To fit bust (in)	30	32	34	36	38	40
Actual bust (cm)	80	85	90	95	101	106
Actual bust (in)	31½	33½	35½	37½	39¾	41¾
Length (cm)	62	62	63	64	65	66
Length (in)	24½	24½	24¾	25¼	25½	26
Sleeve seam (cm)	32	32	32	33	33	34
Sleeve seam (in)	12½	12½	12½	13	1.3	13½

62(62:63:64:65:66)cm
24½(24½:24¾:24¼:25½:26)in
32(32:32:33:33:34)cm
12½(12½:12½:13:13:13½)in
66(71:76:81:87:92)cm
26(28:29¼:31⅞:34¼:36¼)in

BACK

Foundation row: Using a 5mm (US size H/8) crochet hook and Col A, make 110(114:118:124:128:134) chain + 1 chain.

Cont working in rows, turning at end of each row.

Row 1: 1 dc in second ch from hook, 1 dc in each ch to end of row.

(110(114:118:124:128:134) sts)

Row 2: 1 ch, *1 dc in each st to end of row.

Rows 3–10: Work as Row 2.

Sizes 14 and 16 only:

Rep Row 2 a further 2 times.

All sizes:

Row 1: 1 ch, work dec by working next 2 sts tog (dc2tog), *1 dc in each st to last 3 sts, dc2tog, 1 dc in last st.

(108(112:116:122:126:132) sts)

Row 2: 1 ch, 1 dc in each st to end of row.

Rows 3–4: Work as Row 2.

Rep these 4 rows a further 18 times.

(72(76:80:86:90:96) sts)

SHAPE ARMHOLE

Row 1: 1 ch, *1 dc in each st to last 4(4:4:5:5:6) sts, turn.

Row 2: Work as Row 1. *(64(68:72:76:80:84) sts)*

Row 3: 1 ch, dc2tog, *1 dc in each st to last 3 sts, dc2tog, 1 dc in last st. *(62(66:70:74:78:82) sts)*

Row 4: 1 ch, 1 dc in each st to end of row.

Rep Rows 3–4 a further 4(4:4:5:5:6) times.

(54(58:62:64:68:70) sts)

Cont repeating Row 4 only, working in dc patt straight without any further shaping, until work measures 60(60:61:62:63:64)cm/23½(23½:24:24½:24⅞:25)in.

SHAPE SHOULDER

Row 1: Sl st in each of next 6(7:8:8:8:9) sts, *1 dc in each st until last 6(7:8:8:8:9) sts, turn.

Row 2: Sl st in each of next 5(6:7:7:8:8) sts, *1 dc in each st until last 5(6:7:7:8:8) sts.

Break yarn and fasten off.

LEFT FRONT

Foundation row: Using a 5mm (US size H/8) crochet hook and Col A, make 62(64:66:69:71:74) chain + 1 chain.

Cont working in rows, turning at end of each row.

Row 1: 1 dc in second ch from hook, 1 dc in each ch to end. *(62(64:66:69:71:74) sts)*

Row 2: 1 ch, *1 dc in each st to end of row.

Rows 3–10: Work as Row 2.

Sizes 14 and 16 only

Rep Row 2 a further 2 times.

All sizes:

Row 1: 1 ch, dc2tog, 1 dc in each st to end of row.

Row 2: 1 ch, *1 dc in each st to end of row.

(61(63:65:68:70:73) sts)

Rows 3–4: Work as Row 2.

Rep these 4 rows a further 18 times.

(43(45:47:50:52:55) sts)

SHAPE ARMHOLE

Row 1: 1 ch, 1 dc in each st to end of row.

Row 2: 1 ch, 1 dc in each st to last 4(4:5:5:5:6) sts, turn. *(39(41:43:45:47:49) sts)*

Row 3: 1 ch, dc2tog, 1 dc in each st to end of row. *(38(40:42:44:46:48) sts)*

Row 4: 1 ch, 1 dc in each st to end of row.

Rep Rows 3–4 a further 4(4:4:5:5:6) times. *(34(36:38:39:41:42) sts)*

Cont working straight, without any shaping, until work measures 54cm (21¼in), ending with a WS row.

SHAPE NECK

Row 1 (RS): 1 ch, 1 dc in until 16 sts rem, turn.

Row 2: 1 ch, dc2tog, 1 dc in each st to end of row.

Row 3: 1 ch, 1 dc in each st until 3 sts rem, dc2tog, 1 dc in last st.

Row 4: Work as Row 2.

Row 5: Work as Row 3.

Row 6: Work as Row 2.

Row 7: Work as Row 3.

Row 8: Work as Row 2.

Cont working straight in dc patt without any shaping, until work measures 60(60:61:62:63:64)cm/23½(23½:24:24½:24⅞:25)in or same as Back.

SHAPE SHOULDER

Row 1: Sl st in each of next 6(7:8:8:8:9) sts, 1 dc in each st to end of row.

Row 2: 1 ch, 1 dc in each of next 4(5:6:6:7:7) sts.

Break yarn and fasten off.

RIGHT FRONT

Work as given for Left Front, but working three WS buttonhole rows when work measures 30cm (11¾in), 40cm (15¾in) and 50cm (19¾in) as folls:

Buttonhole row (WS): Working towards centre front, 1 dc in each st to last 8 sts, 3 ch, miss 3 sts, 1 dc in each of next 5 sts.

When working next row, work 1 dc in each of 3-chs to pick up these sts.

Cont working Right Front as given for Left Front.

SLEEVES (MAKE 2)

Foundation row: Using a 5mm (US size H/8) crochet hook and Col A, make 58(58:60:60:62:64) chain + 1 chain.

Cont working in rows, turning at end of each row.

Row 1: 1 dc in second ch from hook, 1 dc in each st to end of row. *(58(58:60:60:62:64) sts)*

Row 2: 1 ch, 1 dc in each st to end of row.

Rep Row 2 until work measures 32(32:32:33:33:34) cm/12½(12½:12½:13:13:13¼)in.

SHAPE ARMHOLE

Row 1: 1 ch, 1 dc in each st to last 4 sts, turn.

Row 2: Work as Row 1. *(50(50:52:52:54:56) sts)*

Work dec rows as folls:

Row 3: 1 ch, dc2tog, 1 dc in each st until last 3 sts, dc2tog, 1 dc in last st, turn.

Row 4: 1 ch, 1 dc in each st to end of row.

Rep Rows 3–4 a further 16(16:16:16:17:17) times.

Break yarn and fasten off.

BUTTONHOLE FLOWERS (MAKE 3)

Foundation ring: Using a 5mm (US size H/8) crochet hook and Col C, make 7 chain, join with sl st in first ch to make a ring.

Round 1: 20 dc in centre of ring.

Round 2 (petals): *3 ch, [yo hook twice, insert in next st, pull through, yo, pull through two of the loops, yo, pull through two loops] three times, with four loops still on hook, yo, pull through all four loops, break yarn and pass through rem loop, rejoin yarn in next st; rep from * a further 4 times round ring.

BUTTONS (MAKE 3)

Foundation ring: Using a 5mm (US size H/8) crochet hook and Col B, make a loose slip knot, make 1 chain.

Round 1: 3 dc in slip knot, join rnd with sl st in top of 1ch. *(3 sts)*

Round 2: 1 ch, 2 dc in each st, join rnd with sl st in top of 1ch. *(6 sts)*

Round 3: 1 ch, 1 dc in each st, join rnd with sl st in top of 1ch.

Row 3: 1 ch, [dc2tog] 3 times.

Break yarn and fasten off.

Using a blunt-ended needle or tapestry needle, draw sts tog to form a ball shape.

TO FINISH

Weave in any yarn ends into the wrong side of the fabric so that they are not visible from the right side.

Begin by sewing the shoulder seams together, then sit the sleeveheads into armholes of the front and back pieces, pin them in place and then stitch them together. Finally, sew up the side seams by stitching from the bottom of the garment up to the armhole and then all along the sleeve seam. Weave in any yarn ends. Stitch buttonhole flowers onto Right Front sitting around opening of each buttonhole. Sew these buttons onto the Left Front to match the buttonholes on Right Front.

ADD TRIM

Using your preferred colour – either the main colour or a contrasting shade – add a trim around the edge of your jacket.

With RS facing, beg at bottom of back panel, insert hook and make 3 chain, 2 tr in base of 3ch, *3 tr in space about 2cm (¾in) along; rep from * along bottom edge of garment, work 5 tr in corner, cont up centre front, work 5 tr in corner, cont around neck, work 5 tr in corner, cont down centre front, work 5 tr in corner, cont along bottom of garment to meet first 3ch, join with sl st in top of 3ch.

Repeat around sleeve edges.

+ENLARGED GRANNY SQUARE SWEATER

///

YOU WILL NEED

YARN

Debbie Bliss *Rialto DK*, or a similar double-knitting-weight wool yarn, in four colours:

A 7 x 50g (1¾oz) balls in dark purple (62 Mulberry)
B 2 x 50g (1¾oz) balls in mauve (64 Mauve)
C 2 x 50g (1¾oz) balls in coral pink (55 Coral)
D 2 x 50g (1¾oz) balls in pale blue (60 Sky)

CROCHET HOOK

4mm (US size G/6) crochet hook

OTHER EQUIPMENT

Blunt-ended needle or tapestry needle for weaving in yarn ends and seaming

TENSION

5–6 repeats of 3tr-cluster and 7 rows to 10cm (4in) measured over stitch pattern using a 4mm (US size G/6) crochet hook

ABBREVIATIONS

See page 9

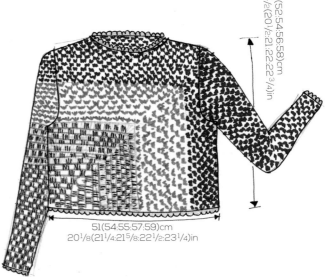

50(52:54:56:58)cm
19½(20½:21:22:22¾)in

51(54:55:57:59)cm
20⅛(21¼:21⅝:22½:23¼)in

SIZE (UK)	8	10	12	14	16
To fit bust (cm)	81	86	91	97	102
To fit bust (in)	32	34	36	38	40
Actual bust (cm)	102	106	110	114	118
Actual bust (in)	40	42	43½	45	46½
Length (cm)	50	52	54	56	58
Length (in)	19½	20½	21	22	22¾
Sleeve seam (cm)	46	46	46	46	46
Sleeve seam (in)	18	18	18	18	18

⁺GRANNY SQUARES

Choose four colours, beg with Col A, 4 ch and join rnd with a sl st. 3 ch (counts as 1 tr), 2 tr in centre of circle; *2 ch (corner space), 3 tr in centre, rep from * a further 2 times, 2 ch then join with a sl st in top of first 3-ch. Break yarn and fasten off.

Round 2: Join Col B in corner space, 3 ch, 2 tr in same space, 1 ch, 3 tr then 1 ch to take you to next corner space, (3 tr, 2 ch, 3 tr). After your final 1 ch, join a with a sl st in top of tch. Break yarn and fasten off.

Round 3: Cont in this patt for all your rnds (you can make your granny square as large as you like): Change to the next colour. Join the new yarn to a corner space and 2 ch, 2 tr in same space. 1 ch, 3 tr in space, *1 ch, (3 tr, 2 ch, 3 tr) in corner sp, 1 ch, 3 tr in sp rep from * to end, finish with a 1 ch and join with a sl st in top of tch.

Cont in this patt. As you work each row the number of sps along each side will inc but work 3 tr in each dividing with a 1 ch and 3 tr, 2 ch, 3 tr in each corner space.

CROCHETING TOGETHER GRANNY SQUARES

To join your granny squares together you can simply sew them together using the mattress stitch method or you can crochet them together. To do this, sit your granny square next to each other, with WS facing.

Step 1 Work as if you were dc along the edge but crochet through sts on both granny square as you work, binding the two squares tog.

Step 2 Once you've finished working along the granny square edges, the seam will look like this from the WS.

Step 3 And the seam will look like this from the RS of your work.

BACK

Foundation row: Using a 4mm (US size G/6) crochet hook and Col A, make 113(117:121:125:129) chain + 3 chain.
Cont working in rows, turning at end of each row.
Row 1: 1 tr in fourth ch from hook, *1 ch, miss 1 ch, 1 tr in next 3 ch; rep from * to end of row, ending with a 1 tr in final 2 ch.
Row 2: 3 ch, *3 tr in 1-ch space, 1 ch; rep from * to end of row, ending with 1 tr in top of tch.
Row 3: 3 ch, 1 tr in first 1-ch space, *3 tr in next 1-ch space, 1 ch; rep from * to last space, 1 tr in final space, 1 tr in top of tch.
Rep Rows 2–3 until work measures 24(26:28:30:32)cm/(9½(10¼:11:11⅞:12½)in).

SHAPE ARMHOLE

Row 1 (RS): Sl st 6 sts across 2 groups of 3 tr; work in stitch pattern until 2 groups of 3 tr rem, turn.
Row 2: Work in stitch pattern to end.
Rows 3–8: 3 ch, miss 2 sts, work in stitch pattern to end of row.
Cont working in stitch pattern without any shaping until work measures 48(50:52:54:56)cm/(18⅞(16$\frac{6}{8}$:20½:21¼:22)in).

SHAPE SHOULDER

Row 1 (RS): Sl st 4(6:8:10:12) sts across 1(1½:2:2½:3) groups of 3-tr; work in st patt until 1(1½:2:2½:3) groups of 3-tr rem, turn.
Rows 2–3: Work in stitch pattern to end to row.
Break yarn and fasten off.

FRONT

Foundation ring: Using a 4mm (US size G/6) crochet hook and Col B, make 4 chain, join with a sl st in first ch to make a ring.
Cont working in rows, turning at end of each row.
Row 1 (RS): 3 ch (counts as first tr), 2 tr in centre of ring, 2 ch, 3 tr in centre of ring, turn.
Row 2: 3 ch, 3 tr in 2-ch space, 2 ch, 3 tr in same ch space, 1 tr in top of 3ch of previous rnd, turn.
Row 3: 3 ch, 2 tr in sp at base of 3ch, 1 ch, in 2-ch space [3 tr, 2 ch, 3 tr], 1 ch, 3 tr in next 1-ch space, turn.
Row 4: 3 ch, 3 tr in next 1-ch space, 1 ch, in corner-sp [3 tr, 2 ch, 3 tr], 1 ch, 3 tr in next 1-ch space, 1 ch, 1 tr in top of tch, turn.
Row 5: 3 ch, 2 tr in ch space at base of 3ch, 1 ch, 3 tr in next 1-ch space, 1 ch, in corner space [3 tr, 2 ch, 3 tr], 1 ch, 3 tr in next 1-ch space, 1 ch, 2 tr in last 1-ch space, turn.
Cont working in granny square stitch patt as set, enlarging square as you work, until square measures 12(13:14:15:16) cm/4¾(5⅛:5½:6:6¼)in.
Change to Col C and cont working in granny square stitch pattern as set until square measures 24(26:28:30:32)cm/9⅜(10¼:11:11⅞:12$\frac{6}{8}$)in, ending with a WS row.

SHAPE ARMHOLE

Change to Col D.
Row 1 (RS): Work until 2 groups of 3-tr rem, 1 tr in centre of next 3-tr group, turn.
Row 2: Work in patt to end of row.
Row 3: Work in patt to last 3-tr group, 2 tr in next ch space, turn.
Row 4: 3 ch, 1 tr in next ch space, work in patt to end of row.
Rep Rows 3 and 4 twice more.
Cont working straight in granny square stitch pattern as set without shaping until square measures 36(39:42:45:48)cm/(14⅛(14⅜:16½:17¾:18⅞)in).
Change to Col A and cont working in granny square stitch pattern as set until square measures 40(42:44:46:48)cm/(14⅞(15⅛:17¼:18⅛:18⅞)in).

Size 16 only

Change to Col A.
Row 1 (RS): Work around square until 23(24:25:26:27)cm/(9(9⅜:9⅞:10¼:10⅝)in) rem of row along top edge, turn.
Row 2: Work back round to end of row.
Break yarn and fasten off.

All sizes

SHAPE NECK

Leaving a gap of 12cm (4⅝in) for neck opening, place a marker at each end.
Rejoin yarn at side edge.
Work each side of neck separately.

Sizes 8, 12 and 16 only

Row 1 (RS): 3 ch, 1 tr in corner space of square, work in st patt for 5(–:6:–:7) 3tr-groups, 2 tr in next sp, turn.
Row 2: 3 ch, 3 tr in next sp, work in st patt to end of row.

Sizes 10 and 14 only

Row 1 (RS): 3 ch, 1 tr in corner space of square, work in st patt for –(6:–:7:–) 3tr-groups, turn.
Row 2: 3 ch, 3 tr in next space, work in patt to end of row.

All sizes

Row 3: 3 ch, 1 tr in corner-sp of square, work in st patt for 4(5:5:6:6) 3tr-groups, turn.
Row 4: 3 ch, 3 tr in next space, work in patt to end of row.
Row 5: 3 ch, 1 tr in corner space of square, work in st patt for 3(4:4:5:5) 3tr-groups, turn.
Row 6: 3 ch, 2 tr in next space, 1 ch, 3 tr in next 1(1:2:2:3) ch-sp, 1 ch, 2 tr in next space, turn.
Row 7: 3 ch, 3 tr in next 1(1:2:2:3) ch space, 1 ch, 1 tr in next space.

Break yarn and fasten off.
With RS facing, rejoin yarn at other side edge.
Row 1: 3 ch, work in st patt to shoulder edge.
Rows 2–3: Work in st patt as set to end of row.
Rows 4–10: Work as Rows 1–7 as given for previous side of neck.

SHAPE FRONT SIDE

Match this to the other side edge of the Front. It's quite tricky to get perfect as you're crocheting in a different direction.
With RS facing, rejoin Col A yarn at bottom of work.
Row 1: 3 ch, work approx 28(30:32:34:36:38)cm/(11(11⅞:12⁶⁄₈:13⅜:14⅛:15)in) of st patt, matching other edge, turn.
Row 2: Work in st patt to end of row.
Row 3: Work as Row 1 for approx 25(27:29:31:33)cm/(9⅞(10⅝:11½:12⅛:13)in), turn.
Row 4: Work as Row 2.
Row 5: Work as Row 1 for 22(24:26:28:30)cm/(8⅝(9½:10¼:11:11⅞)in), turn.
Row 6: Work as Row 2.
Rows 7–10: Work in st patt without any shaping.
Break yarn and fasten off.

PLAIN SLEEVE (MAKE 1)

Foundation row: Using a 4mm (US size G/6) crochet hook and Col A, make 49(49:53:53:57) chain + 3 chain.
Row 1: 1 tr in fourth ch from hook, *1 ch, miss 1 ch, 1 tr in each of next 3 sts: rep from * to end of row, ending with 1 tr in final 2 sts.
Row 2: 3 ch, *3 tr in 1ch-sp, 1 ch; rep from * to end of row, ending with 1 tr in top of tch.
Row 3: 3 ch, 1 tr in first 1-ch space, *3 tr in next 1-ch space, 1 ch; rep from * to end of row, ending with 1 tr in final sp and 1 tr in top of tch.
Cont working in granny square stitch pattern as set until work measures approx 6cm (2¼in), ending with a WS row.
Inc row 1 (RS): 3 ch, 2 tr in first 1-ch space, *3 tr in next 1-ch space, 1 ch; rep from * to end of row, ending with 3 tr in final sp, turn.
Inc row 2 (WS): 3 ch, 1 tr in base of 3-ch, 1 ch, *3 tr in next 1-ch space, 1 ch; rep from * to end of row, ending with 2 tr in last st.
Cont working in granny square stitch pattern as set until work measures approx 12cm (4⅝in), ending with a WS row.
Note number of rows worked from last inc row.
Work Inc Rows 1–2 once more.
***Working inc rows at regular intervals, cont working in granny square stitch pattern as set until same number of rows have been worked as bet pairs of inc rows, ending with a WS row.
Work Inc Rows 1–2 once more.
Rep from *** a further 4 times.
Cont working in granny square stitch pattern without shaping until Sleeve measures 45cm (17¾in) from foundation row.
Break yarn and fasten off.

SHAPE SLEEVEHEAD

Row 1 (RS): Miss 2 reps, rejoin yarn to centre tr of next 3-tr group, 3 ch, work to same point at other end of row, turn.
Row 2: Work in st patt as set.
Row 3: 4 ch, miss first group of either 2-tr or 3-tr, work in st patt, miss last group, 1 tr in top of tch.
Row 4: Work in st patt as set to end of row.
Rep Rows 3–4 a further 8 times.
Rep Row 3 once more.
Break yarn and fasten off.

STRIPED SLEEVE (MAKE 1)

Work as given for Plain Sleeve, but using Col B until work measures 33cm (13in).
Change to Col C and cont until work measures 46.5cm (18¼in) or stripe is equal to depth of Col C stripe on Front.
Change to Col D and cont until work measures 60cm (23⅝in) or stripe is equal to depth of Col C stripe on Front.
Change to Col A and cont until Sleeve has been completed.

TO FINISH

Weave in any yarn ends into the wrong side of the fabric so that they are not visible from the right side.
Lightly steam each garment piece before sewing together.
Seam together the Back and Fronts at the shoulders.
Set the sleeveheads into the armholes. Pin these in place first before sewing just to make sure the garment pieces don't slip around and change position.
Sew up the side seams all the way from the bottom of the garment up to the underarm and along the sleeve seam.

ADD TRIM

Add the trim around the cuffs, neckline and bottom of sweater using Col C.
Begin at the back of the garment, 3 ch in one of the gaps, work 2 tr in same gap, *3 tr in next 1ch-sp; rep from * all the way round, join with a sl st to top of 3ch.

PATCHWORK STITCH SWEATER

YOU WILL NEED

YARN
6(7:8) x 100g (3½oz) hanks of Ginger Twist Studio *Sheepish DK*, or a similar double-knitting-weight wool yarn, in shade pale pink (Barbapapa)

CROCHET HOOK
4.5mm (US size 7) crochet hook

OTHER EQUIPMENT
Blunt-ended needle or tapestry needle for weaving in yarn ends and seaming

TENSION
2 fans and 5 rows to 10cm (4in) measured over main fan stitch pattern

ABBREVIATIONS
See page 9

SPECIAL ABBREVIATIONS
ttr-group = work 3 triple treble in next double crochet until one loop of each remains on hook, yarn over and draw through all four loops on hook.

double-ttr-group = work 3 triple trebles in same double crochet as last group until one loop of each remains on hook (four loops on hook), miss 5 double crochet, in next double crochet work 3 triple treble until one loop of each remains on hook, yarn over and draw through all seven loops on hook.

dtrX (double treble "X" shape – worked over 3 sts) = yarn over twice, insert hook in next stitch, yarn over, draw loop through, yarn over, draw through two loops, miss next stitch, yarn over, insert hook in next stitch, yarn over, draw loop through, [yarn over, draw through two loops] four times, 1 chain, yarn over, insert hook half way down stitch just made where lower "legs" join, yarn over, draw loop through, [yarn over, draw through two loops] twice.

cluster4 = work 3 treble over stem of treble just worked but leaving last loop of each treble on hook, then work fourth treble as indicated leaving last loop as before (five loops on hook), yarn over and through all five loops.

SIZE (UK)	S (6–8)	M (10–12)	L (14–16)
To fit bust (cm)	76–81	86–91	97–102
To fit bust (in)	30–32	34–36	38–40
Actual bust (cm)	80	90	100
Actual bust (in)	31½	35½	39½
Length (cm)	53	56	56
Length (in)	21	22	22
Sleeve seam (cm)	45	47	49
Sleeve seam (in)	17¾	18½	19¼

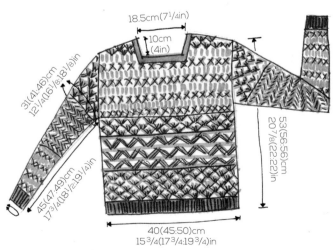

18.5cm(7¼in)

10cm (4in)

31(41:46)cm 12¼(16¼:18⅛)in

45(47:49)cm 17¾(18½:19¼)in

53(56:56)cm 20⅞(22:22)in

40(45:50)cm 15¾(17¾:19¾)in

BACK

Begin by working the rib, which is crocheted horizontally across body.

Foundation row: Using a 4.5mm (US size 7) crochet hook, make 15 chain.

Cont working in rows, turning at end of each row.

Row 1: 1 dc in third ch from hook (counts as 2 dc sts), 1 dc in each ch to end of row.

Row 2: 1 ch, sl st in each of next 14 sts.

Row 3: 1 ch, 1 dc in each sl st to end of row.

Rep Rows 2–3 a further 62(69:76) times.

Break yarn and fasten off.

With RS facing, rejoin yarn and work 81(89:97) sl st evenly across top of rib.

Break yarn and fasten off.

FAN STITCH PATTERN

With RS facing, rejoin yarn in first sl st of rib edging.

Row 1: 1 ch, *miss 3ch, 9 tr in next st, miss 3ch, 1 dc in next st; rep from * to end of row.

Row 2: 3 ch (counts as first tr), 1 tr in next st, *5 ch, miss 9tr-group, work V-st [1 tr, 1 ch, 1 tr] in next dc; rep from * ending with 5 ch, miss last 9tr-group, 2 tr in last dc, miss tch, turn.

Row 3: 3 ch (counts as first tr), 4 tr in first st, *miss 5ch, 1 dc in fifth tr of group **, 9 tr in sp at centre of next V-st; rep from * ending last rep at **, 5 tr in top of tch, turn.

Row 4: 3 ch, miss 5tr, V-st in next dc, *5 ch, miss 9tr-group, V-st in next dc; rep from * ending 2 ch, sl st to top of tch, turn.

Row 5: 1 ch, miss sl st, 1 dc in next st, *9 tr in sp at centre of next V-st**, miss next 5ch, 1 dc in fifth dc of group in row below; rep from * ending last rep at **, 1 dc in first ch of tch, turn.

Rep Rows 2–5 once more.

Rep Rows 2–3 once more.

Work final row of fan st patt as folls:

Next row (WS): In place of 5ch bet V-sts [2 ch, sl st to fifth tr of group, 2 ch].

ZIGZAG STITCH PATTERN

Row 1 (RS): 1 ch, 1 dc in each st to end of row, loosing 1(3:5) sts across row by evenly spacing and working decs, turn.

Row 2: 1 ch, 1 dc in each st to end of row, turn.

Row 3: 5 ch (counts as first ttr), miss 3dc, work 1ttr-group in next dc, *1 double-ttr-group, 5 ch; rep from * to last 3dc, in same dc as last group work 3ttr until one loop of each rems on hook (four loops), 1ttr in last dc until five loops rem on hook, yo and draw through all five loops, turn.

Row 4: 1 ch, 1 dc in top of first group, 5 dc in 5ch-sp, *1 dc in top of next group, 5 dc in next 5ch-sp; rep from * to last group, 1 dc in fifth of 5ch at beg of previous row, turn.

Row 5: 1 ch, work 1 dc in each dc to end of row, turn.

Rows 2–5 form the zigzag pattern.

Rep Rows 2–5 twice more.

Size Small

Work Row 2 once more.

Sizes Medium and Large

Work Rows 2–5 once more.

All sizes

Work fan st Rows 1–6, inc sts across first row to 81(89:97) sts.

Place a marker at each end of last row for Sleevehead position. * * *

HOT CROSS BUN STITCH PATTERN

Row 1 (RS): 1 ch, *1 dc in each st to end of row, turn.

Row 2: 4 ch (counts as 1 dtr), miss first st, *dtr over next 3 sts; rep from * ending 1 dtr in last st, miss tch, turn.

Row 3: 4 ch (counts as 1 tr and 1 ch), *work tr3tog in next 1ch-sp **, 2 ch; rep from * ending last rep at **, 1 ch, 1 tr in top of tch, turn.

Row 4: 1 ch, 1 dc in first st, 1 dc in next ch, *1 dc in next cl, 1 dc in each of next 2 ch; rep from * to end, turn.

Rows 2–4 form the Hot Cross Bun pattern.

Rep Rows 2–4 until work measures 19cm (7½in) from start of Hot Cross Bun st patt, ending with a WS row.

SHOULDER SHAPING

Rows 1–2: Work in fan st patt to end of row.

Row 3: Sl st to centre of first fan, work in fan st patt to centre of last fan, turn.

Row 4: Sl st to centre of second fan, work in fan st patt to last two fans, ending with a sl st in centre of fan below, turn.

Row 5: Work as Row 5 of fan st patt across 5(6:7) complete fans.

Row 6: Work as Row 6 of fan st patt across 5(6:7) complete fans.

Break yarn and fasten off.

FRONT

Begin by working the rib, which is crocheted horizontally across body.

Foundation row: Using a 4.5mm (US size 7) crochet hook, make 15 chain.

Work as given for Back until ***.

With RS facing, work in hot cross bun st patt until work measures 43(46:46)cm/(17(18:18)in) from foundation row.

SHAPE NECK

Cont working in hot cross bun st patt as folls:

Row 1 (RS): Work 8(10:12) hot cross bun sts, turn, leaving rest of row unworked.

Cont working in hot cross bun st patt as set on these sts only for a further 5cm (2in).

Dec 1 st at neck edge on each of next 3 rows.

Cont working in fan st patt.

Work Rows 1–5 then Rows 2–5 so two fan st reps have been worked.

Next row (WS): Work in fan st patt to end of row.

SHAPE SHOULDER

Row 1: Sl st to centre of first fan, work in fan st patt to end of row.

Row 2: Work in fan st patt to centre of last fan, turn.

Row 3: Work 1(1½:2) fans.

Break yarn and fasten off.

With RS facing, miss 18 sts for neck opening, rejoin yarn.

Row 1: Work in fan st patt to centre of last fan, turn

Row 2: Work in fan st patt to centre of last fan, turn.

Row 3: Work 1(1½:2) fans.

Break yarn and fasten off.

SLEEVES (MAKE 2)

Foundation row: Using a 4.5mm (US size 7) crochet hook, make 51(59:67) chain.

Work as given for Back until ***.

Cont working in hot cross bun st until 19(21:23)cm/ (7½(8½:9)in) of hot cross bun st has been worked, ending with a WS row, but at the same time inc 1 st at each end of next row every foll fourth row.

Cont to work cl st, but at the same time inc 1 st at each end of every fourth row until work measures 36(41:46) cm/(14(16:18)in) wide.

Row 1 (RS): 3 ch, miss 1 st, work 1 tr in next st, *3 ch, miss 2 ch, work c l4, placing fourth tr in next ch; rep from * to last 2 sts, 3 ch, work c l4 placing fourth tr in last ch, turn.

Row 2: 3 ch, 1 tr in next 3-ch space, *3 ch, work c l4 placing fourth tr in next 3-ch space; rep from * to end placing final tr in top of ch at beg of previous row, turn.

Rep Row 2, cont to inc as above until work measures 34(36:38)cm/13¼(14:15)in, ending with a WS row.

Cont working in fan st patt.

Rep fan st Rows 1–5 until 10cm (4in) of fan st has been worked.

Break yarn and fasten off.

SLEEVE RIBS (MAKE 2)

The sleeve ribs are worked separately as folls:

Foundation row: Using a 4.5mm (US size 7) crochet hook, make 15 chain.

Row 1: 1 dc in third ch from hook, 1 dc in each ch to end of row.

Row 2: Sl st in each of next 14 sts.

Row 3: 1 ch, 1 dc in each sl st to end of row.

Rep Rows 2–3 a further 21(28:35) times.

Break yarn and fasten off.

Stretch each rib to fit along the bottom edges of the sleeves and stitch in place.

TO FINISH

Weave in any yarn ends into the wrong side of the fabric so that they are not visible from the right side.

Seam together the Back and Fronts at the shoulders.

ADD NECKLINE

Rejoin yarn to lefthand shoulder seam, 1 ch, work 20 dc evenly down left side of Front, 16 dc across centre Front, 20 dc up right side of Front and 35 dc evenly across Back, join with a sl st in first dc.

Rounds 1–3: 1 ch, 1 dc in each st to end of rnd, join with a sl st in first dc.

Break yarn and fasten off.

Pin the top of the sleeves across the top of the Front and Back over the shoulder seam, so each side of the sleeve meets the contrast yarn marker. Stitch the sleeve in place. Sew the Back and Fronts together along the side seams, stitching from the bottom edge of the garment up to the underarm, then down along the underarm Sleeve seams to the rib cuffs.

FRILLED EDGE CARDI

///

YOU WILL NEED

YARN

Quince & Co *Chickadee*, or a similar double-knitting-weight wool yarn, in four colours:

A 7(8:8:8:9) x 50g (1¾oz) hanks in pale blue (Bird's Egg)
B 1(1:1:1:1) x 50g (1¾oz) balls in pale yellow (Carrie's Yellow)
C 1(1:1:1:1) x 50g (1¾oz) balls in pale pink (Dogwood)
C 1(1:1:1:1) x 50g (1¾oz) balls in dark red (Pomegranate)

OTHER MATERIALS

Seven 2cm (⅞in) diameter buttons

CROCHET HOOK

4mm (US size G/6) crochet hook

OTHER EQUIPMENT

Blunt-ended needle or tapestry needle for weaving in yarn ends and seaming

TENSION

7½ V-sts and 10 rows to 10cm (4in) measured over V-st stitch pattern using a 4mm (US size H/8) crochet hook

ABBREVIATIONS

See page 9

SPECIAL ABBREVIATIONS

starting shell = 1 chain, 1 double crochet in base of chain, miss 1 stitch, 5 treble in next stitch, miss 1 stitch.
shell st = 1 double crochet, miss 1 stitch, 5 treble in next stitch, miss 1 stitch.

SIZE (UK)	8	10	12	14	16
To fit bust (cm)	81	86	91	97	102
To fit bust (in)	32	34	36	38	40
Actual bust (cm)	85	91	96	102	107
Actual bust (in)	34	36	38	40	42
Length (cm)	60	60	62	64	66
Length (in)	23½	23½	24½	25	26
Sleeve seam (cm)	44	44	46	46	46
Sleeve seam (in)	17½	17½	18	18	18

44(44:46:46:46)CM
17⅜(17⅜:18⅛:18⅛:18⅛)in

60(60:62:64:66)CM
23⅝(23⅝:23⅝:23¾:26)in

43(45.5:48:51:53.5)CM
16⅞(17⅞:18⅞:20⅛:21)in

BACK

Foundation row: Using a 4mm (US size H/8) crochet hook and Col A, make 90(96:102:108:114) chain + 1 chain.

Cont working in rows, turning at end of each row.

Row 1 (RS facing): 1 tr in fourth ch from hook, *miss 2 ch, work a V-st of [1 tr, 1 ch, 1 tr] in next ch; rep from * to last 3 ch, miss 2 ch, 1 tr in last ch, turn.

Row 2: 4 ch, 1 tr in first st, *V-st in second tr of next V-st; rep from * until 1 tr and tch rem, miss 1 tr and 1 ch, 1 tr in next ch, turn.

Cont repeating Row 2 throughout Back but working Row 2 a further 26(26:28:29:30:32) times using Col A. Change to Col B.

Next row: Work as Row 2.

Change to Col A, rep Row 2 a further 2 times.

SHAPE ARMHOLE

Using Col A, cont repeating Row 2 throughout break yarn and rejoin in second arm of first V-st, work across row to second arm of last full V st, turn.

Cont working in st patt as set, work next 6 rows as folls:

Row 1: Using Col C, 4 ch but don't make tr in same st as patt, instead go straight to first V-st. Work row to last V-st , make V-st without central ch, 1 tr in final st.

Rows 2–5: Using Col A, work as Row 1.

Row 6: Using Col D, work as Row 1.

Using Col A , work a further 12 rows without shaping. Break yarn and fasten off.

SHAPE SHOULDER

Rejoin yarn, miss 7 sts at edge, 3 ch, V-st in second arm of next V-st, cont working across row in offset V-st patt to last 3 V-sts, 3 ch, 1 dc in second arm of next V-st. Break yarn and fasten off, turn.

Rejoin yarn to second arm of second V-st, 3 ch, V-st in second arm of next V-st, cont in patt to last 3 V-sts, 2 ch, 1 dc in second arm of next V-st.

Break yarn and fasten off, turn.

Rejoin yarn in first arm of second V-st, 1 dc in each tr and ch to last V-st.

Break yarn and fasten off.

FRONT (MAKE 2)

Foundation row: Using a 4mm (US size 7) crochet hook and Col A, make 57(60:63:66:69) chain + 1 chain.

Work as for Back to armhole shaping.

SHAPE ARMHOLE

Using Col A, cont repeating Row 2 throughout break yarn and rejoin in second arm of first V-st, work to end of row.

Cont working in st patt as set, work next 6 rows as folls:

Row 1: Using Col C, work to last V-st, make V-st without central ch, 1tr in final st.

Row 2: Using Col A, 4 ch but don't make tr in same st as in patt, instead go straight to first V-st, work to end of row, turn.

Row 3: Work as Row 1.

Row 4: Work as Row 2.

Row 5: Work as Row 1.

Row 6: Using Col D, work as Row 1.

Work one more row in V-st patt without shaping.

SHAPE NECKLINE

Row 1: V-st in each of next 8(8:8:9:9) V-sts only, turn.

Row 2: 3 ch, work tr2tog in next st and first arm of first V-st, V-st in patt as set to end, turn.

Row 3: V-st in each V-st to last V-st, tr2tog in last arm of last V-st and final st.

Row 4: Rep Row 3.

Row 5: Work 6 rows of V-st patt without shaping.

Shape shoulders as for Back, but working at sleeve edge only.

Break yarn and fasten off.

SLEEVES (MAKE 2)

Using a 4mm (US size 7) crochet hook and Col A, make
48(48:48:51:51) chain + 1 chain.

Row 1 (RS facing): 1 tr in fourth ch from hook, *miss
2 ch, work a V-st of [1 tr, 1 ch, 1 tr] in next ch; rep from *
to last 3 ch, miss 2 ch, 1 tr in last ch, turn.

Row 2: 4 ch, 1 tr in first st, *V-st in second tr of next
V-st; rep from * to last 1 tr and tch, miss 1 tr and 1 ch,
1 tr in next ch, turn.

Rep Row 2 a further 38 times but work incs in foll rows:

Row 3: Work in patt as set until eighth V-st, inc by
working 2 V-sts in one V-st (1 V-st in each arm), work in
patt as set to end or row.

Row 8: Work in patt as set until eighth V-st, work extra
V-st bet V-sts 8 and 9, work in patt as set to end of row.

Row 13: Work in patt as set until nineth V-st, 2 V-sts in
next V-st, work in patt as set to end of row.

Row 18: Work in patt as set until tenth V-st, 2 V-sts in
next V st, work in patt as set to end of row.

Row 22: Work in patt as set until tenth V-st, 2 V-sts in
next V-st, work in patt as set to end of row.

Row 26: Work in patt as set until eleventh V-st, 2 V-sts
in next V-st, work in patt as set to end of row.

Row 30: Work in patt as set until eleventh V-st, 2 V-sts
in next V-st, work in patt as set to end of row.

Row 34: Work in patt as set until twelfth V-st, 2 V-sts in
next V-st, work in patt as set to end of row.

Row 38: Work in patt as set until twelfth V-st, 2 V-sts in
next V-st, work in patt as set to end of row.

Break yarn and fasten off.

SHAPE ARMHOLE

Rejoin yarn to third V-st, work in patt set until 2 V-sts
rem at end of row.

Work a further 16 rows, working this 4-row dec patt
a further 4 times.

Work dec at alt ends of row so over these 16 rows, 12 sts

will have been dec – six on each side:

Row 1: Dec (over last 2 V-sts of row, miss first arm of
first V-st, 1 tr in second arm, 1 ch, 1 tr in first arm of
second V-st, tr in usual final st).

Row 2: Work as Row 1.

Row 3: Work as Row 1.

Row 4: Work in patt as set without shaping.

Next row: 1 ch, 1 dc in each st and space to end of row.
Break yarn and fasten off.

TO FINISH

Weave in any yarn ends into the wrong side of the fabric
so that they are not visible from the right side.

Seam together the Back and Fronts at the shoulders.

Sit the sleeve heads into the armholes. Pin these in place
first before sewing just to make sure the garment pieces
don't slip around and change position. Sew the Back and
Fronts together along the side seams, stitching from the
bottom edge of the garment up to the underarm, then
down along the underarm Sleeve seams.

ADD COLLAR

Row 1: Using Col A, join yarn at the centre Front, 1 ch,
work dc evenly around neckline, turn.

Cont working in rows, turning at end of each row.

Row 2: Working in back loop only 2 ch, 1 htr in each of
next 5 sts, 2 htr in next st, * 1 htr in each of next 6 sts,
2 htr in next st; rep from * to end of row, turn.

Row 3: 2 ch, 1 htr in each of next 6 sts, 2 htr in next st,
*1 htr in each of next 7 sts, 2 htr in next st; rep from
* to end of row, turn.

Row 4: Using Col D, 2 ch, 1 htr in each of next 7 sts,
2 htr in next st, *1 htr in each of next 8 sts, 2 htr in next
st; rep from * to end of row, turn.

Row 5: Using Col A, 2 ch, *1 htr in next st; rep from
* to end of row, turn.

Row 6: Using Col C, 2 ch, 1 htr in each of next 9 sts,

2 htr in next st, *1 htr in each of next 10 sts, 2 htr in next st; rep from * to end of row, turn.

Row 7: Using Col A, 2 ch, *1 htr in next st; rep from * to end of row, turn.

Row 8: Using Col B, 2 ch, 1 htr in each of next 12 sts, 2 htr in next st, *1 htr in each of next 13 sts, 2 htr in next st; rep from * to end of row, turn.

Row 9: Using Col A, work a starting shell and then rep the shell st all the way around, 1 dc in final st. Break yarn and fasten off.

ADD CUFFS (WORK AROUND BOTTOM OF EACH SLEEVE)

Round 1: Using Col D, join yarn at bottom of Sleeve, 2 ch, 1 htr in each of next 3 sts, 2 tr in next st, *1 htr in each of next 4 sts, 2 tr in next st; rep from * to end of round. Join rnd with a sl st in top of 2-ch.

Cont working in rnds, with RS always facing.

Round 2: Using Col C, 2 ch, 1 htr in each of next 4 sts, 2 tr in next st, *1 htr in each of next 5 sts, 2 tr in next st; rep from * to end of rnd, join with a sl st in top of 2-ch.

Round 3: Using Col B, 2 ch, 1 htr in each of next 5 sts, 2 tr in next st, *1 htr in each of next 6 sts, 2 tr in next st; rep from * to end of rnd, join rnd with a sl st in top of 2-ch.

Round 4: Using Col A, work a starting shell and then rep the shell st all way round, join with a sl st in top of 2-ch. Break yarn and fasten off.

ADD TRIM AT BOTTOM OF CARDIGAN

Row 1: Using Col D, join yarn at centre front of Left Front, 3 ch , work tr evenly across bottom of cardigan to centre front of Right Front.

Row 2: 3 ch, 1 tr in each st to end of row. Break yarn and fasten off.

ADD BUTTON BAND

Beg working button band on Left Front.
Cont working in rows, turning at end of each row.

Row 1: Using Col B and with RS facing, re-join yarn at top of centre front on Left front, ch3, tr evenly all the way down front and across bottom edge of trim, turn.

Row 2: 1 ch, 1 dc in each st to end of row.

Row 3: 3 ch, 1 tr in each st to end of row. Break yarn and fasten off.

ADD BUTTONHOLE BAND

Sit your buttons along this button band to determine where you would like them. Place markers on Right Front at position of each button so you can work your buttonholes at the preferred places.

Row 1: Using Col B and with RS facing, re-join yarn at bottom of centre front on Right Front, 3 ch, tr evenly all the way up front to top edge, turn.

Row 2: 1 ch, *1 dc in each st until next button place marker, *2 ch, miss 2 sts; rep from * to last marker, 1 dc in each st to end of row.

Row 3: 3 ch, 1 tr in each st to end of row. Break yarn and fasten off.

Sew buttons on Left Front button band to match buttonholes on Right Front.

+KIMONO JACKET

///

YOU WILL NEED

YARN

Jamieson's of Shetland *DK* or a similar double-knitting-weight yarn in five colours:

A 9(9:10:10:11) x 25g (⅞oz) balls in bright pink (629 Lupin)

B 8(8:9:9:10) x 25g (⅞oz) balls in purple (585 Plum)

C 2(2:2:2:3) x 25g (⅞oz) balls in pale blue (655 China Blue)

D 2(2:2:2:3) x 25g (⅞oz) balls in yellow (400 Mimosa)

E 3(3:3:3:4) x 25g (⅞oz) balls in orange (308 Tangerine)

CROCHET HOOK

4mm (US size G/6) crochet hook

OTHER EQUIPMENT

Blunt-ended needle or tapestry needle for weaving in yarn ends and seaming

TENSION

17 sts and 12 rows to 10cm measured over spike stitch pattern using 4mm (US size G/6) crochet hook

SIZE (UK)	8	10	12	14	16
To fit bust (cm)	81	86	91	97	102
To fit bust (in)	32	34	36	38	40
Actual bust (cm)	106	111	116	121	126
Actual bust (in)	41¾	43¾	45¾	47¾	49¾
Length (cm)	48	48	49	49	50
Length (in)	19	19	19¼	19¼	19¾
Sleeve seam (cm)	18	18	19	19	20
Sleeve seam (in)	7	7	7½	7½	8

+SPIKE STITCH

Step 1 Begin by working in your usual stitch patt up to the point where you would like to make the spike stitch. Insert your hook into the space created in the row or rows below.

Step 2 Feed your crochet hook with slightly more yarn than usual so that the stitch isn't too tight and your work does not pucker. Finish working your stitch as normal.

Step 3 Work to the end of your row and you will see your spike stitches.

+ BOBBLE STITCH

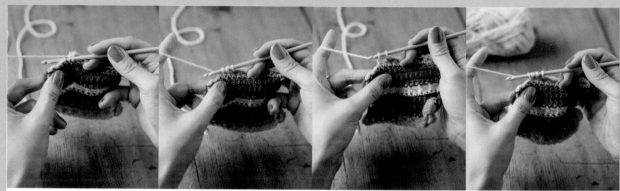

STEP 1 Begin your stitch with yrh then insert your hook into the next stitch.

STEP 2 Yrh then draw through the stitch.

STEP 3 Yrh then pass through two of the loops sitting on your hook.

STEP 4 Instead of finishing this stitch off, yrh and work another stitch into the same stitch. You will now have three loops sitting on your hook.

STEP 5 Repeat these steps until you have worked five stitches into the same stitch, so you should now have six loops in total sitting on your crochet hook.

STEP 6 Yrh and draw through all six loops.

STEP 7 Finish off by working 1 dc in the next stitch along, fastening your bobble in place.

STEP 8 Work to the end of the row and you will be able to see all your lovely bobbles from the RS of your work,

BACK

Foundation row: Using a 4mm (US size G/6) crochet hook and Col E, make 90(93:96:99:102) chain + 2 chain. Cont working in rows, turning at end of each row.

Row 1: 1 dc in third ch from hook, 1 dc in each ch to end of row. *(90(93:96:99:102) sts)*

Row 2: 2 ch (counts as first dc), *work bobble st in next st, 1 dc in next st; rep from * to end of row.

Row 3: Change to Col A, 2 ch (counts as first dc), *1 dc in each st to end of row.

Row 4: Work as Row 3.

Rows 5–6: Change to Col B, work as Row 3.

Rows 7–8: Change to Col A, work as Row 3.

Row 9: Change to Col D, 1 ch, 1 dc in next st to end of row.

Row 10: 2 ch (counts as first dc), *work bobble st in next st, 1 dc in next st; rep from * to end of row.

Rows 11–16: Work as Rows 3–8.

Rows 17–18: Change to Col C, work as Rows 9–10.

Rows 19–24: Work as Rows 3–8.

Row 25: Change to Col A, 3 ch (counts as first tr), 1 tr in each of next 2 sts, *1 ch, 1 tr in each of next 3 sts; rep from * to end of row.

Row 26: 3 ch, 1 tr in each of next 2 sts, *miss ch st, 1 tr in each of next 3 sts; rep from * to end of row.

Row 27: Change to Col B, 3 ch, 1 tr in first st, *miss ch, 1 tr in next st, work 1 spike stitch (sp st) in ch 2 rows below, 1 tr in next st; rep from * to end of row.

Row 28: Work as Row 26.

Row 29: Change to Col A, 3 ch, 1 sp st in ch 2 rows below, 1 tr in next st, *miss 1 st, 1 tr in next st, 1 sp st in ch 2 rows below, 1 tr in next st; rep from * to end of row.

Row 30: Work as Row 26.

Rows 27–30 form the spike stitch pattern. Cont working in this patt until work measures 25(25:26:26:26)cm/ (10(10:10½:10½:10½)in).

SHAPE RAGLAN

Cont working in sp st patt as folls, but at the same time working decs by missing sts:

Row 1 (RS): 3 ch, miss 1 st, work in patt to last 2 sts, miss 1 st, 1 tr in last st.

Row 2: 3 ch, miss 2 sts, work in patt to last 3 sts, miss 2 sts, 1 tr in last st.

Row 3: Work as Row 1.

Row 4: Work as Row 2.

Rep these 4 dec rows until 18(21:24:21:24) sts rem. Break yarn and fasten off.

LEFT FRONT

Foundation row: Using a 4mm (US size G/6) crochet hook and Col E, make 44(47:50:53:56) chain + 2 chain. Work in patt as given for Back until raglan shaping.

SHAPE RAGLAN

Cont working in sp st patt as folls, but at the same time working decs by missing sts:

Row 1 (RS): 3 ch, miss 1 st, work in patt to end of row.

Row 2: Work in patt to last 3 sts, miss 2 sts, 1 tr in last st.

Cont working in sp st patt, rep the last 2 rows until 15(18:21:18:21) sts rem. Break yarn and fasten off.

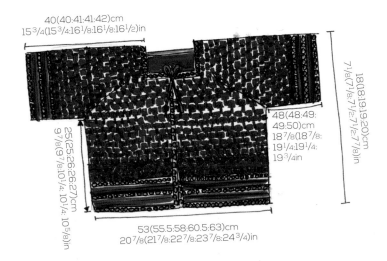

40(40:41:41:42)cm
15³/4(15³/4:16¹/8:16¹/8:16¹/2)in

25(25:26:26:27)cm
9⁷/8(9⁷/8:10¹/4:10¹/4:10⁵/8)in

53(55.5:58:60.5:63)cm
20⁷/8(21⁷/8:22⁷/8:23⁷/8:24³/4)in

48(48:49:49:50)cm
18⁷/8(18⁷/8:19¹/4:19¹/4:19³/4)in

18(18:19:19:20)cm
7¹/8(7¹/8:7¹/2:7¹/2:7⁷/8)in

RIGHT FRONT

Foundation row: Using a 4mm (US size G/6) crochet hook and Col E, make 44(47:50:53:56) chain + 2 chain. Work as patt for Back until Raglan shaping.

SHAPE RAGLAN

Cont working in sp st patt as folls, but at the same time working decs by missing sts:

Row 1 (RS): Work to last 2 sts, miss 1 st, 1 tr in last st.
Row 2: 3 ch, miss 2 sts, work to end of row.
Cont working in sp st patt, rep the last 2 rows until 15(18:21:18:21) sts rem.
Break yarn and fasten off.

SLEEVES (MAKE 2)

Foundation row: Using a 4mm (US size G/6) crochet hook and Col E, make 85(88:91:94:97) chain + 2 chain.
Cont working in patt as given for Back until end of Row 30.
Cont working in sp st patt until work measures 20(20:21:21:21)cm/(8(8:8½:8½:8½)in), ending at the same point in the patt rep as on Back and Fronts.

RAGLAN SHAPING

Cont working in sp st patt as folls, but at the same time working decs by missing sts:

Row 1: 3 ch, miss 1 st, work to last 2 sts, miss 1 st, 1 tr in last st.
Row 2: 3 ch, miss 2 sts, work to last 3 sts, miss 2 sts, 1 tr in last st.
Row 3: Work as Row 1.
Row 4: Work as Row 2.
Rep the last 4 dec rows a further 9(9:9:10:10) times, then work as folls for the different sleeves, cont in the spike st patt:

LEFT SLEEVE

Row 1: 3 ch, miss 1 st, work in patt to end of row.
Row 2: Work to last 3 sts, miss 2 sts, 1 tr in last st.
Row 3: Work as Row 1.
Row 4: Work as Row 2.
Break yarn and fasten off.

RIGHT SLEEVE

Row 1: Work to last 3 sts, miss 2 sts, 1 tr in last st.
Row 2: 3 ch, miss 1 st, work in patt to end of row.
Row 3: Work as Row 1.
Row 4: Work as Row 2.
Break yarn and fasten off.

TO FINISH

Weave in any yarn ends to the wrong side of your work so they are not visible on the right side. Stitch up the raglan seams, joining the Left and Right Fronts to the Sleeves and then the Sleeves to the Back. Finally, sew up the side seams, stitching upwards from the bottom of the garment, sewing the Left and Right Fronts and Back together, all the way up to the underarm and then down along the sleeve seam, joining the Sleeves together.

ADD EDGE TRIM

With right side facing, using a 4mm (US size G/6) crochet hook and Col E, chain 2 on the edge of one of the centre fronts. Double crochet all along this edge until you reach either the bottom of the garment or the neckline depending on which side you are working on, turn. Chain 3, *work bobble st in next st, 1 dc in next stitch; repeat from * to the end of the centre front. Break yarn and fasten off. Repeat along the other centre front edge.

ADD NECKLINE TRIM

With right side facing, using a 4mm (US size G/6) crochet hook and Col E, chain 2 on the centre front of the Right Front, work dc all along this edge until you reach the centre front of the Left Front, turn. Chain 3, *work bobble stitch in next stitch, work dc in next stitch; repeat from * to your initial chain 2. Break yarn and fasten off.

MAKE TIES (MAKE TWO)

Using a 4mm (US size G/6) crochet hook and Col E, make 60 chain + 1 chain.

Row 1: 1 dc in second ch from hook, *1 dc in each ch to end of row, turn.
Row 2: 2 ch (counts as first dc), *1 dc in each st to end of row. Break yarn and fasten off.
Fasten one tie to the top edge of both the Left and Right Fronts on the wrong side of the fabric.

+YARN INFORMATION

A yarn is specified for each of the designs in this book. If you use the recommended yarn, you just need to pick your preferred shade. If you use a different yarn, compare tensions to ensure the finished results will not differ wildly. There are standard yarn weights recognised throughout the industry. Hand-knit and crochet yarns range from 2ply laceweight through to superbulky. Within any category there is a degree of tolerance, so it is important to check the tension of each yarn against that given in a pattern. The spinner's recommend tension needle or hook size may vary from the pattern. If so, always go with the pattern designer's recommendation.

BC GARN SEMILLA ORGANIC DK
100% wool; 160m (175 yd) per 50g (1¾oz) ball; recommended tension 22 sts and 30 rows to 10cm (4in) measured over st st using 4–4.5mm (US size 6–7) knitting needles; *http://garn.dk*

BC GARN SEMILLA ORGANIC GROSSO
100% wool; 80m (87½ yd) per 50g (1¾oz) ball; recommended tension 15 sts and 20 rows to 10cm (4in) measured over st st using 6–7mm (US size 10–10½) knitting needles; *http://garn.dk*

DEBBIE BLISS RIALTO DK
100% merino wool; 105m (115 yd) per 50g (1¾oz) ball; recommended tension 22 sts and 30 rows to 10cm (4in) measured over st st using 4mm (US size 6) knitting needles; *http://debbieblissonline.com*

DROPS ALPACA 4PLY
100% alpaca; 167m (182½ yd) per 50g (1¾oz) ball; recommended tension 23 sts and 30 rows to 10cm (4in) measured over st st using 2.75–3.5mm (US size 2–4) knitting needles; *http://garnstudio.com*

GINGER TWIST STUDIO SHEEPISH DK
100% wool; 225m (246yd) per 100g (3½oz) hank; recommended tension 20–22 sts to 10cm (4in) measured over st st using 4mm (US size 6) knitting needles; *http://www.gingertwiststudios.com*

JAMIESON'S OF SHETLAND DK
100% wool; 75m (82 yd) per 25g (⅞ oz) ball; recommended tension 25 sts and 32 rows to 10cm (4in) measured over st st using 3.75mm

(US size 5) knitting needles; *http://www.jamiesonsofshetland.co.uk*

JAMIESON'S OF SHETLAND SPINDRIFT
100% wool; 105m (115 yd) per 25g (⅞oz) ball; recommended tension 30 sts and 32 rows to 10cm (4in) measured over st st using 3.25mm (US size 3) knitting needles; *http://www.jamiesonsofshetland.co.uk*

JC RENNIE SUPERSOFT 4PLY
100% wool; 246m (269 yd) per 50g (1¾oz) ball; recommended tension 28 sts and 36 rows to 10cm (4in) measured over st st using 3mm (US size 3) knitting needles; *http://www.knitrennie.com*

JILL DRAPER MAKES STUFF HUDSON
100% merino wool; 219m (239½ yd) per 113g (4oz) hank; recommended tension 16–20 sts to 10cm (4in) measured over st st using 5mm (US size 8) knitting needles; *https://www.etsy.com/uk/shop/jilldrapermakesstuff*

MISTI ALPACA CHUNKY
100% alpaca; 100m (109 yd) per 100g (3½oz) ball; recommended tension 14 sts to 10cm (4in) measured over st st using 6mm (US size 10) knitting needles; *http://mistialpaca.com*

ORKNEY ANGORA ST MAGNUS DK
50% angora, 50% wool; 200m (218 yd) per 50g (1¾oz) ball; recommended tension 20 sts to 10cm (4in) measured over st st using 3.5mm (US size 4) knitting needles; *http://orkneyangora.co.uk*

QUINCE & CO CHICKADEE
100% wool; 166m (181½ yd) per 50g (1¾oz) ball; recommended tension 26 sts to 10cm (4in) measured over st st using 3.25mm (US size 3) knitting needles; *http://quinceandco.com*

QUINCE & CO OSPREY
100% wool; 155m (169½ yd) per 50g (1¾oz) ball; recommended tension 14 sts to 10cm (4in) measured over st st using 5.5mm (US size 9) knitting needles; *http://quinceandco.com*

RICO COLOUR TOUCH
98% wool, 2% polyester; 90m (98 yd) per 100g (3½oz) ball; recommended tension 12 sts and 16 rows to 10cm (4in) measured over st st using 9mm (US size 13) knitting

needles; *http://www.rico-design.de*

RICO CREATIVE COTTON ARAN
100% cotton; 85m (93 yd) per 50g (1¾oz) ball; recommended tension 17 sts and 22 rows to 10cm (4in) measured over st st using 4–5mm (US size 6–8) knitting needles; *http://www.rico-design.de*

RICO ESSENTIALS COTTON DK
100% cotton; 130m (142 yd) per 50g (1¾oz) ball; recommended tension 22 sts and 28 rows to 10cm (4in) measured over st st using 4mm (US size 6) knitting needles; *http://www.rico-design.de*

ROWAN HANDKNIT COTTON
100% cotton; 85m (93 yd) per 50g (1¾oz) ball; recommended tension 19–20 sts and 28 rows to 10cm (4in) measured over st st using 4–4.5mm (US size 6–7) knitting needles; *http://www.knitrowan.com*

ROWAN ORIGINAL DENIM
100% cotton; 92m (100 yd) per 50g (1¾oz) ball; recommended tension 20 sts and 32 rows to 10cm (4in) measured over st st using 4mm (US size 6) knitting needles; *http://www.knitrowan.com*

ROWAN PURE WOOL 4PLY
100% wool; 160m (175 yd) per 50g (1¾oz) ball; recommended tension 28 sts and 36 rows to 10cm (4in) measured over st st using 3.25mm (US size 3) knitting needles; *http://www.knitrowan.com*

ROWAN MOHAIR HAZE
30% wool, 70% mohair; 102m (111½ yd) per 25g (⅞ oz) ball; recommended tension 28 sts and 36 rows to 10cm (4in) measured over st st using 3mm (US size 2–3) knitting needles; *http://www.knitrowan.com*

WOOL AND THE GANG
SHINY HAPPY COTTON
100% cotton; 142m (155 yd) per 100g (3½oz) ball; recommended tension 16 sts to 10cm (4in) measured over st st using 5mm (US size 8) knitting needles; *http://www.woolandthegang.com*

YEOMAN YARNS CANNELLE 4PLY
100% cotton; 850m (929½ yd) per 245g (8½ oz) cone; recommended tension 33 sts and 44 rows to 10cm (4in) measured over st st using 2.75mm (US size 2) knitting needles; *http://yeoman-yarns.co.uk*

⁺MEET THE TEAM

PUBLISHING DIRECTOR Jane O'Shea
COMMISSIONING EDITOR Lisa Pendreigh
EDITORIAL ASSISTANT Harriet Butt
PATTERN CHECKER Luise Roberts
CREATIVE DIRECTOR Helen Lewis
ART DIRECTION AND DESIGN Claire Peters
PRODUCTION DIRECTOR Vincent Smith
PRODUCTION CONTROLLER Tom Moore

PHOTOGRAPHER Laura Edwards
PHOTOGRAPHER'S ASSISTANTS Alex
Davenport, Suzie Howell & Kim Lightbody
STYLIST Verity Pemberton
HAIR AND MAKE-UP ARTISTS Terri Capon
& Danni Hooker
MODELS Rebecca Arnold at Nevs, Claudia
Devlin at Nevs, Emily Green at M&P and
Drew Gregory Fountain at FM
HAND MODEL Chinh Hoang

First published in 2015 by Quadrille Publishing Ltd
Pentagon House
52–54 Southwark Street
London SE1 1UN
www.quadrille.co.uk

Quadrille
craft

www.quadrillecraft.com

Quadrille is an imprint of Hardie Grant
www.hardiegrant.com.au

British Library Cataloguing-In-Publication Data
A catalogue record for this book is available from the British Library.

ISBN 978 184949 547 9

10 9 8 7 6 5 4 3 2 1

Printed in China.

If you have any comments or queries regarding the instructions in this book, please contact us at enquiries@quadrille.co.uk.

I would like to say a huge thank you to everyone at Quadrille for all their hard work and for making such a lovely book that I feel incredibly proud to have my name on the front of. Thank you to Lisa for giving me the opportunity to write this book and to Claire for making it look so lovely. I know there are so many people who have worked on this book and made it what it is, so thank you so much to you all. To Laura, Verity and everyone who was involved in the photoshoots – thank you for getting such beautiful photographs and for making the days fun. I couldn't be happier with this book and I'm so lucky to have had such amazing and creative people work on it.

Thank you to all the crocheters, Victoria Stott, Joanna Wilkinson, Helen Barber and Camilla Fraser, who helped me to create all the projects in this book and for being so reliable and hard working. A huge thank you also to the lovely Jess from Ginger Twist Studio for the gorgeous pink yarn used for the Patchwork Stitch Jumper.

My biggest thank you goes to Richard and to my lovely parents, Joanna and Martin, for their continuous, unending encouragement and support in whatever I set my mind to.